DANTON'S DEATH

Though he was born at the beginning of the nineteenth century and wrote only three plays during his short life, Georg Büchner is considered one of the forefathers of modern theatre. *Danton's Death,* his first play, written at the age of twenty-one, was completed in five weeks in an effort to raise money to escape the police authorities that were hounding him for his revolutionary activities. Büchner died of typhus two years later in 1837. Like his other plays, *Woyzeck* and *Leonce and Lena,* *Danton's Death* was never staged during his lifetime, remaining unperformed until 1902.

In 1982 the playwright Howard Brenton was commissioned to provide a version of the play for the National Theatre. His text follows the recently published definitive German edition and is wholly faithful to Büchner's original.

The print on the cover shows 'A Revolutionary Committee during the Terror' and is reproduced by courtesy of the Mansell Collection.

Georg Büchner

DANTON'S DEATH

A new version by Howard Brenton
From a translation by Jane Fry

METHUEN · LONDON

A Methuen Paperback

First published as a paperback original in 1982
by Methuen London Ltd,
11 New Fetter Lane, London EC4P 4EE
Translation copyright © 1982 by Howard Brenton
Chronology copyright © 1979 by Michael Patterson
Original work entitled DANTONS TOD
ISBN 0 413 51260 6
Set in IBM 10 Point Journal by 𝍫 Tek-Art, Croydon, Surrey
Printed in Great Britain by Richard Clay
(The Chaucer Press) Ltd, Bungay, Suffolk

Karl Georg Büchner

1813   Born on 17 October in Goddelau in the Grand Duchy of Hesse-Darmstadt, a state of some 700,000 inhabitants. For generations the Büchners had been barber-surgeons and Georg's father was a doctor in the service of the autocratic Grand Duke.

1816   Family moved to Darmstadt.

1822   Schooling, first in private school, then (from 1825)
-31   at Darmstadt Gymnasium.

1831   Studied natural science (zoology and comparative
-33   anatomy) in Strasbourg. First encounter with radical student politics. Became secretly engaged to 'Minna' Jaeglé, daughter of the pastor with whom he lodged.

1833   To comply with regulations, regretfully returned to
-34   Hesse to continue studies at the University of Giessen, a mediocre institution with some 400 students and no buildings of its own. Suffered attack of meningitis. Helped to found revolutionary 'Society of Human Rights' both here and later in Darmstadt.

1834   In uneasy collaboration with the liberal agitator, Pastor Weidig, issued illegal pamphlet DER HESSISCHE LANDBOTE (THE HESSIAN COURIER), urging the peasants to revolt, especially against heavy taxation. August: arrest of one of Büchner's associates. Büchner himself denounced as author of DER HESSISCHE LANDBOTE, but lack of evidence and his own confident assertion of innocence delayed his arrest. Returned home to Darmstadt and consolidated 'Society of Human Rights' there.

1835   In five weeks secretly wrote DANTONS TOD (DANTON'S DEATH), a tragedy depicting Danton's disillusionment with the French Revolution. March: fled to Strasbourg to avoid arrest, and never returned to Germany or engaged in political activities again. Continued studies (philosophy and comparative anatomy). July: with the help of the influential writer Gutzkow, DANTONS TOD was published in an expurgated edition, the only work of Büchner's to be published during his life-time. Translated two plays by Victor Hugo: MARIE TUDOR and LUCRÈCE BORGIA. Worked on his unfinished novella LENZ about a Storm and Stress poet on the verge of insanity. From now on suffered frequent depressions and from the effects of overwork.

1836   Became member of the 'Société d'histoire naturelle' at Strasbourg and read his paper (in French) on the nervous system of the barbel-fish. Wrote his delicately ironical romantic comedy LEONCE UND LENA for a literary competition but submitted it too late. It was returned unread. Probably began work on WOYZECK and wrote his non-extant drama PIETRO ARETINO while still in Strasbourg. September-October: became Doctor of Philosophy at Zurich University and, after a trial lecture on the cranial nerves of fish, was appointed Lecturer in Natural Sciences (Comparative Anatomy).

1837   January: apparently on the point of completing WOYZECK. 19 February: died of typhus after 17 days' illness.

1850   First edition of Büchner's *Collected Works* in German (did not contain WOYZECK).

1875   WOZZECK first published in periodical *Mehr Licht*.

1879   First 'critical' edition of *Complete Works* (contained unreliable version of WOZZECK).

1895   Premiere of LEONCE UND LENA in a private performance.

1902   Premiere of DANTONS TOD in Berlin.

1913   Premiere of WOZZECK in Munich.

1922   Bergemann publishes critical edition of Büchner's works (title of play now recognised for first time as WOYZECK).

1923   Publication of Alban Berg's opera WOZZECK.

1925   Premiere of Berg's opera in Berlin.

1927   First translation of Büchner into English by Geoffrey Dunlop.

1967   Definitive Hamburg Edition of Büchner's works (first philologically accurate version of WOYZECK).

Danton's Death

Characters

GEORGES DANTON
LEGENDRE
CAMILLE DESMOULINS
HÉRAULT-SÉCHELLES *Deputies of the National*
LACROIX *Convention*
PHILIPPEAU
FABRE D'ÉGLANTINE
MERCIER
THOMAS PAINE

ROBESPIERRE
SAINT-JUST *Members of the Committee of*
BARÈRE *Public Safety*
COLLOT D'HERBOIS
BILLAUD-VARENNES

CHAUMETTE, *Procurator of the Paris Commune*
DILLON, *a general*
FOUQUIER-TINVILLE, *Public Prosecutor*

HERMAN *Presidents of the Revolutionary*
DUMAS *Tribunal*

AMAR *Members of the Committee of*
VOULAND *General Security*

PARIS, *a friend of Danton*
SIMON, *a theatre prompter*
LAFLOTTE
JULIE, *Danton's wife*
LUCILE, *Camille Desmoulin's wife*
SIMON'S WIFE
ROSALIE
ADELAIDE *Grisettes*
MARION

Men and women of the people, prostitutes, Deputies, tumbril drivers, hangmen, etc.

Act One

Scene One

HÉRAULT-SÉCHELLES *with a* GROUP *of* WOMEN *at the card table.*

DANTON *and* JULIE *some distance from them.* DANTON *sitting on a stool at* JULIE's *feet.*

DANTON. Look at that beautiful woman playing a beautiful game of cards. Yes, she knows the game. They say she gives her husband her heart but other men her diamond. You women, you can trick a man into falling in love with a lie.

JULIE. Do you trust me?

DANTON. How can I tell? We know very little about each other. We are lumbering, thick-skinned animals, we reach out our hands to touch but the strain is pointless, we blunder about rubbing our coarse skins up against each other. We are very much alone.

JULIE. You know me, Danton.

DANTON. What we call knowing. You have dark eyes, curly hair, fine skin and you call me 'dear Georges'. But! (*He indicates her forehead and eyes.*) There, what lies behind there? Ha! Our senses are crude. We'd have to crack open the tops of our skulls to really know each other, tear out each other's thoughts from the fibre of the brain.

A WOMAN (*to* HÉRAULT). What are you doing with your fingers?

HÉRAULT. Nothing!

A WOMAN. Don't hold your thumb up like that. It's disgusting.

HÉRAULT. Look, doesn't it remind you of something?

DANTON. No, Julie, I love you like the grave.

JULIE (*turning away*). The grave. Oh, thank you.

DANTON. No, listen! It's said peace and the grave are as one.
So, I lie in your lap and already I am underground. My sweet
grave, your lips are my passing bells, your voice my death
knell, your breast my mound of earth, your heart my coffin.

A WOMAN. You've lost!

HÉRAULT. An affair of the heart. And like all affairs of the
heart, it costs money.

A WOMAN. So. Like a deaf mute, you declare love with your
fingers?

HÉRAULT. Why not? Some say fingers are more eloquent than
words. I wove my way into the affections of a queen of
playing cards. My fingers were princes. Like in the fairy tale,
they turned into spiders and span a web. You, madam, were
the fairy godmother. But it all went wrong, the Queen was
always in childbirth, popping out one knave after another.
What a game! I'd never let my daughter play it. The kings fall
on top of the queens with no sense of shame at all and the
knaves come thick and fast.

CAMILLE DESMOULINS *and* PHILIPPEAU *come on.*

Philippeau! Why the tragic eyes? Did someone tear your red
cap? Did St Jacques give you a black look as he went up to
heaven? Or did it just rain at the guillotining and you got a
rotten seat and couldn't see a thing?

CAMILLE. He's parodying Socrates. You know: one day
Socrates found Alcibiades sulking and said 'Alcibiades! Did
you lose your shield on the battlefield? Were you beaten in a
race or a sword fight? Or did someone just sing and play the
zither better than you?' Oh, you learned and classical
republicans! You should try the romance of our guillotine.

PHILIPPEAU. Twenty more victims fell today. We were wrong
when we said the Hébertists went to the scaffold because
their opposition was impetuous, not systematic enough. The
real reason may be that the Committee of Public Safety could
not let men stay alive who, even for one week, were more
feared than themselves.

HÉRAULT. The Decemvirs want to put us back before the flood. St. Just wants us to crawl on all fours again, so Robespierre can put dunces caps on our heads and sit us up on school benches; and drum the catechism of a new Supreme Being into us, concocted from the mechanical theories of a clock-maker philosopher from Geneva.

PHILIPPEAU. And to that end they do not flinch from adding a few noughts to Marat's account book of those to be murdered. How long must we be dirty and bloody as new-born children, with coffins for cradles and severed heads for toys? We must progress. The Committee of Clemency must begin work, the Deputies who were expelled must be re-instated.

HÉRAULT. The Revolution has reached the stage of transformation. The Revolution must end, the Republic must begin. In the constitution of our state, rights must replace duties. The well-being of the individual must replace virtue and self-defence replace punishment. Every man must speak his mind and act according to his nature. What a man may or may not be, how wise or stupid, cultivated or uncultivated, how good or bad — is no concern of the state. We are all fools and we have no right to suppress each other's folly. Every man must be free to enjoy life in his own way, save that no man may enjoy himself at another's expense, or obstruct the pleasure of anyone else.

CAMILLE. The state must be a transparent robe, clear as water, that clings close to the body of the people. Every ripple of the sinews, every tensing of the muscles, every swelling of the veins must be imprinted upon its form. Never mind if the figure be beautiful or ugly, let it be as it is, we have no right to cut and tailor the garment to our wishes. We'll rap the knuckles of those who want to throw a nun's veil round the bare shoulders of our beloved sinner, France.

We want naked gods, Bacchanite women, Olympic games and from melodious lips, the songs of a cruel, limb-loosening love. We don't want to prohibit the Romans from sitting in the corner cooking turnips. We just want them to stop giving us gladiatorial bloodbaths.

Let divine Epicurus, and Venus with her beautiful behind, be the doorkeepers of our Republic, not Saints Marat and Chalier.

Danton, you will launch the attack in the Convention.

DANTON. I will, you will, he will. 'If we live to see day dawn', as the old women say. An insight: in one hour's time, sixty minutes will have passed.

CAMILLE. That's a crushingly obvious remark, Danton —

DANTON. Oh everything is obvious, no? For example, who will put this visionary splendour into practice?

PHILIPPEAU. We will. And all decent people.

DANTON. Ah! That 'and', a long word, it sets us and them far apart. The road is long, will the decent be there with us at its end? I think not, they'll have collapsed a long way back, out of breath. You can lend money to decent people, you can marry your daughters to them, but that's all.

CAMILLE. If you don't believe in decency, why begin the struggle at all?

DANTON. I find those sanctimonious jumped up Catos repulsive, whenever I see them I want to kick them in the teeth. I can't help it, it's the way I'm made.

He rises.

JULIE. Are you going?

DANTON (*to* JULIE). I must. They are wearing me down with their politics.

As he leaves.

Parting words. A prophecy. The statue of liberty has not yet been cast, the furnace is red hot, we may all yet burn our hands.

He goes off.

CAMILLE. Let him go. Do you think he'll keep *his* hands off, when the time comes?

HÉRAULT. No. But only to kill time, the way you play chess.

Scene Two

In the street.

SIMON *and his* WIFE.

SIMON (*beats his wife*). Panderess! Pimping clap pill! You dose on two legs! You maggot-packed old bitch! You apple rotten with sin!

WIFE. Help me! Help me!

PEOPLE (*running in*). Tear 'em apart! Tear 'em apart!

1ST CITIZEN. Who is the old drunk?

A MAN. Simon, he's a prompter in the theatre.

1ST CITIZEN. Prompts his wife too, does he?

SIMON. Unhand me Romans! I want to smash that walking skeleton, that vestal virgin.

WIFE. Vestal virgin? That'll be the day.

SIMON. From off thy shameless shoulder I will tear
      The cloth to lay thy withered carcass bare.
You bed of a whore, lechery nests in every wrinkle.

They are separated.

1ST CITIZEN. Old man, what's the matter?

SIMON. Where's my daughter, my little girl? Girl? No, not the name for what she is. Is she a woman? Oh no, that's not what she is. I've not got the breath for the name.

2ND CITIZEN. Good thing. The name would be 'Brandy'.

SIMON. Old Virginius, cover your face
      Your women told you lies
      Now raven shame perches on your head
      Pecking out your eyes.
Give me a knife, Romans!

He falls to the ground.

WIFE. He's a decent man. It's just that with the brandy, two legs aren't enough.

2ND CITIZEN. Then he'll have to walk on his third leg.

WIFE. He just falls down.

2ND CITIZEN. Dear oh dear, that gone limp too?

SIMON. You are the vampire's tooth, you suck my heart's blood —

WIFE. Let him be, he'll be all right in a moment.

1ST CITIZEN. So what's it all about?

WIFE. Well, I was sitting out on the step, for the sun. See, we've got no wood for a fire —

2ND CITIZEN. Use your husband's nose.

WIFE. And, well, my daughter went down to stand on the corner. She's a good girl, she looks after her parents —

SIMON. She admits it!

WIFE. Judas! You'd have no trousers at all, if men didn't take down theirs with your daughter. You're no father, you're a barrel of brandy. Do you go thirsty? We work with all our parts, why not *that* part? I laboured with mine, to bring her into the world. It hurt me, let hers hurt now. For her mother's sake, eh? Let hers hurt too! Why not?

SIMON. Lucrece! Give me a knife, Romans.

1ST CITIZEN. Yes a knife. But not for the whore, what's she done? Nothing. It's her hunger that whores and begs. A knife for them who buy the flesh of our wives and children. A knife for the rich who whore with the daughters of the people! Your bellies cling to your spines with hunger, theirs groan and bulge. Your coats have holes, theirs have fur. You have hard skin on your hands, their hands are velvet. Ergo! You work, they do not. Ergo! What you earn, they steal. Ergo! If you want to get back a few of the coppers they stole from you, you have to whore and beg. They are the scum of the earth. Ergo! Kill them.

2ND CITIZEN. There is not a drop of blood in their veins not sucked from ours. They told us 'Kill the aristocrats, they are wolves!' We hanged the aristocrats from the lanterns. They said 'The King eats your bread'. We killed the King. They said

'The Girondins are starving you'. We carried the Girondins to the guillotine. But who wears the clothes of the dead? They do! Our legs are still bare and we're freezing. We'll make our own trousers from skin torn from their thighs, we'll melt down their fat and warm ourselves up with a good, rich soup. Death to all with no holes in their coats!

1ST CITIZEN. Death to all who read and write!

2ND CITIZEN. Death to all who run away abroad!

ALL (*shouting*). Death! Death!

Some of them drag forward a YOUNG MAN.

A FEW VOICES. He's got a handkerchief!
                       An aristo!
                       Hang him on the lantern!
                       To the lantern!

2ND CITIZEN. He doesn't blow his nose with his fingers! To the lantern!

A lantern is lowered.

YOUNG MAN. Gentlemen, I —

2ND CITIZEN. No gentlemen here! To the lantern!

A FEW VOICES (*singing*). Don't lie in the ground
                       The worms will eat you there
                       So hang up hang up hang up
                       Hang up in the air.

YOUNG MAN. Mercy!

3RD CITIZEN. It's only a game! A twist of rope round your neck for a second. We have mercy, you do not. You murder us for all our lives, murder by work. We hang on the rope and jerk for sixty years. But now we're cutting ourselves free. To the lantern!

YOUNG MAN. All right, go ahead! I am pleased to be of service, though I doubt if I'll throw much light on the problem.

CROWD. Oh, bravo! Bravo!

A FEW VOICES. Let him go!

He disappears.

Enter ROBESPIERRE *accompanied by* WOMEN *and* SANS CULOTTES.

ROBESPIERRE. What is this, citizens?

3RD CITIZEN. What do you think it is? The people's cheeks are still white. The drops of blood from August and September aren't enough. The guillotine's too slow. We need a downpour.

1ST CITIZEN. Our wives and children cry for bread. We're going to feed them with aristocratic meat. Death to all with no holes in their coats!

ALL. Death! Death!

ROBESPIERRE. In the name of the law!

1ST CITIZEN. What is the law?

ROBESPIERRE. The will of the people.

1ST CITIZEN. We are the people and what do we want? No more law. Ergo our will is law. Ergo in the name of the law there is no more law.

A FEW VOICES. Silence for Aristides!
                Silence for the Incorruptible!

A WOMAN. Listen to the Messiah sent to elect and judge. He will smite the wicked with his sword. His eyes are the eyes of election his hands the hands of judgement.

ROBESPIERRE. Poor virtuous people! You do your duty, you sacrifice your enemies. People, you are great, amid flashes of lightning and to peals of thunder, you reveal yourself. But, good people, do not wound your own body, do not murder yourself in your rage. You are strong, only by your own self-destruction can you fall. Your enemies know that. But your legislators keep watch. Their eyes are infallible, they guide your hands and from the hands of the people there can be no escape. Come with us to the Jacobin Club. Your brothers open their arms to you, we will put your enemies on trial for their lives.

MANY VOICES. To the Jacobins!
                        Long live Robespierre!

All go off, except SIMON *and his* WIFE.

SIMON. Woe is me, deserted!

He tries to get up.

WIFE. There.

She supports him.

SIMON. Alas my Baucis, you heap the coals upon my head.

WIFE. Just stand up!

SIMON. You turn away? Ah, can you forgive me Portia? Did I
      hit you? That wasn't me. I was mad.
            His madness is poor Hamlet's enemy.
            Then Hamlet does it not; Hamlet denies it.
      Where is our daughter? Where's my little Suzanne?

WIFE. Down on the corner.

SIMON. We'll go to her. Come wife, virtuous wife.

Both go off.

Scene Three

The Jacobin Club.

A LYONNAIS. The brothers of Lyons pour out their
      indignation into your hearts. We do not know if the tumbril
      Ronsin rode to the guillotine was the hearse of liberty, but we
      do know that the murderers of Chalier still walk the earth as
      if they will never lie in a grave. Have you forgotten that Lyons
      is a stain on the ground of France, a stain that must be blotted
      out by the corpses of the monarchists and traitors? Have you
      forgotten that Lyons is the whore of Kings and can only wash
      away her sores in the waters of the Rhone? Have you forgotten
      that this revolutionary river must make Pitt's fleet in the
      Mediterranean founder on the corpses of aristocrats? Your

mercy murders the Revolution. Every breath an aristocrat draws is the death rattle of liberty. Only a coward dies for the Republic, a Jacobin kills for it. Know this: if you falter, if we no longer find in you the resolution of the men of the 10th of August and September and the 31st of May, then, as with the suicide of the patriot Gaillard, all that is left to us is — Cato's dagger.

Applause and confused shouts.

A JACOBIN. We'll drink hemlock with you like Socrates!

LEGENDRE (*climbs up onto the platform*). Forget Lyons. Look nearer home. They who wear silk coats and trousers, who drive in coaches, they who sit in the boxes of theatres and talk like the Dictionary of the Academy, still find their heads stuck firmly to their necks. Their confidence has returned. Now they joke and say 'let's give Chalier and Marat a double martyrdom — and guillotine their statues'.

Violent commotion in the Assembly.

A FEW VOICES. They're dead men! Your tongue guillotines them!

LEGENDRE. Let the blood of the saints be upon them! I ask the members of the Committee of Public Safety present, when did your ears go deaf —

COLLOT D'HERBOIS (*interrupts him*). And I ask you, Legendre, whose voice gives breath to such thoughts, so you dare speak them? Who is behind you? It is time to tear off the masks. The cause has its effect, the cry its echo, the reason its consequence. The Committee of Public Safety knows revolutionary logic better than you, Legendre. Don't worry. The statues of the Revolution's saints will not be defiled. Like Medusa's head they will turn the traitors to stone.

ROBESPIERRE. I demand to speak.

JACOBINS. Silence. Silence for the Incorruptible!

ROBESPIERRE. We waited only for this cry of outrage before we spoke. Our eyes were open, we saw the enemy advance but we did not sound the alarm, we allowed the people to keep

watch and they did not sleep, they armed themselves. We
flushed the enemy from hiding, we forced him to show himself
and now he stands exposed in the clear light of day, now you
can cut him down, you have only to look at him and he is dead.
I told you once before, understand: the enemies of the Republic
are in two factions, two camps. Under banners of different
colours, by widely different routes, they hasten toward the
same goal. One of these factions is destroyed. In their
arrogance, their conceited madness, they accused the most
tried and tested Patriots, so to rob the Republic of its strongest
arms. They declared war on the deity and on private property,
but their violent excess was a diversion to help the kings. They
parodied the lofty drama of the Revolution in order to discredit
it. Hébert's triumph would have tipped the Republic into chaos,
to the delight of the despots. Well, the sword of the law has
fallen on that traitor. But does that worry the foreigners?
No, why should it when there are criminals of another kind
to work for them? We have achieved nothing for we have yet
another faction to destroy. It is the opposite of the first. It
urges us to weakness. Its battle-cry is 'Mercy!' And its tactic?
To take away the weapons of the people and the strength of
the people and deliver them, naked and cowed, into the
hands of the kings of Europe. The weapon of the Republic is
terror. The strength of the Republic is virtue. Virtue, because
without it terror is destructive, terror, because without it
virtue is impotent. When terror flows from virtue it is
justice itself, swift, strong and unswerving. They say terror is
the weapon of tyranny, and that our government therefore
resembles a tyranny. Of course it does. But only in as much
as the sword in the hand of a fighter for freedom resembles
the sword of a slave, fighting for a king. The despot rules his
bestial serf through terror. As a despot he has that right. You
are the founders of the Republic. You, too, have the right to
crush, through terror, the enemies of liberty. The
revolutionary government is the despotism of liberty against
tyranny.

'Have mercy on the royalists!' some shout. Mercy for
criminals? No! Mercy for the innocent, mercy for the weak,

mercy for the unfortunate, mercy for mankind. The protection of society is only for the peaceful citizen. In a republic only republicans are citizens, royalists and foreigners are enemies. To punish the oppressors of mankind is a privilege, to pardon them, barbarism. Any sign of false compassion is a sign of hope for England and Austria.

And now, not content with disarming the people, there are those who seek to poison the holy source of the Republic's strength with vice. That is the most devious, dangerous and abominable attack on liberty. Vice is the aristocracy's mark of Cain. In a Republic it is more than a moral, it is a political crime. The libertine is an enemy of the state, the more he seems to serve liberty, the greater the danger. The most dangerous citizen is he who would rather wear out a dozen red caps than do one good deed.

Whom do I mean? Just think of those who once lived in attics and now drive in carriages and fornicate with former marchionesses and baronesses. We may well ask, whence came this wealth? Did they rob the people or shake the golden hands of kings? You see them! These 'tribunes of the people' parading the vice and luxury of the old court, these marquies and counts of the Revolution marrying rich wives, giving lavish banquets, gambling, waited upon by servants, wearing sumptuous clothes. We may well be amazed when we hear them spout their fancy phrases and clever witticisms and congratulate themselves on their 'good taste'. Recently we have seen in our newspapers a parody of Tacitus. I could reply by quoting Sallust and speak of the Cataline Conspiracy. But no, the portraits are complete.

No treaty, no truce for the men who robbed the people and go unpunished, for whom the Republic was a financial swindle and the Revolution a business. Terrified, they are trying to douse the Revolution's fire. I hear them say 'We are not virtuous enough to be so terrible. Oh philosophical legislators pity our weakness, I dare not confess I am full of vice, so I say to you instead, do not be so cruel'.

Be calm, you virtuous people, be calm, patriots, tell your brothers in Lyons how the sword of justice does not sleep in the hands to which you entrusted it. We will give the Republic a great example.

General applause.

MANY VOICES. Long live the Republic, long live Robespierre!

PRESIDENT. The session is closed.

Scene Four

A street.

LACROIX *and* LEGENDRE.

LACROIX. Do you know what you've done, Legendre? Do you know whose head you've knocked off, with your 'statues'?

LEGENDRE. A few dandies, a few fine ladies, that's all.

LACROIX. You're a shadow that murders the body that casts it.

LEGENDRE. What do you mean?

LACROIX. Collot said it clear enough.

LEGENDRE. Who listens to him? He was drunk, again.

LACROIX. Out of the mouths of babes, now out of the mouths of drunks, the truth. Whom do you think Robespierre meant by Cataline?

LEGENDRE. Well?

LACROIX. It's simple. The atheists and ultras have gone to the scaffold. But the people are still barefoot in the streets, crying for shoes made from the skins of the aristocrats. The guillotine's a thermometer, Robespierre cannot allow it to cool. A few degrees down, and the Committee of Public Safety can look for a resting place in the Place de la Revolution.

LEGENDRE. What has my metaphor of the statues to do with that?

LACROIX. Don't you see? You've made the counter-revolution
    official and public. Now the Decemvirs will have to act, you've
    forced their hand! The people are a minotaur that must have
    its corpses or it will turn and gobble them up.

LEGENDRE. Where's Danton?

LACROIX. How do I know? Putting the Venus de Milo together
    bit by bit from all the tarts in the Palais Royal. 'Working on
    his mosaic' he calls it. Who knows what limb he's on now?
    What a cruel joke of nature, to parcel beauty out in little bits,
    like Medea did to her brothers, burying the fragments in
    many bodies. Let's go to the Palais Royal.

They both go off.

Scene Five

A room.

DANTON *and* MARION.

MARION. No, leave me alone, at your feet, like this. I want to tell
    you a story.

DANTON. You could put your lips to better use.

MARION. No, leave me. My mother was a good woman, she told
    me chastity was a great virtue. When people who came to the
    house began to talk about certain things, she'd send me out
    of the room. If I asked what they meant, she'd say I ought to
    be ashamed of myself. When she gave me a book to read, there
    were always pages torn out. She didn't pull pages out of the
    Bible though, that was holy, I could read all of that. But there
    were things in the Bible I didn't understand. I didn't like to
    ask anyone, so I brooded on them, alone. Spring came. All
    around me I felt something going on I had no part in. I was
    lost in my own world, a strange feeling, there was a strange
    atmosphere around me, it almost choked me. I'd lie on my bed
    and look at my body, I'd feel like I was double, then I'd merge
    back into one.

Then, a young man came to the house. He was good looking
and he said extraordinary things: I didn't understand but he
made me laugh. My mother invited him a lot and that suited
us both. In the end we said why sit side by side in two chairs,
when we can lie side by side between two sheets? I enjoyed
that much more than his conversation, and if the greater of
two pleasures is yours for the taking, why not take it? We
did, again and again, in secret. It was lovely. But I began to
change. I became a sea, devouring everything, moved by
tremendous tides, even in its depths. All men's bodies merged
into one, his or any man's. That's how I'm made, can we help
how we are made?

At last he realised. One morning he kissed me as if he wanted
to choke me, he held his arms tight around my neck. I was
terrified. Then he let me go and laughed. He said he didn't
want to spoil my fun. My body was all the finery I had, I'd
need it, it would be torn and dirty and worn out sooner than I
knew. He left. I still didn't understand. That evening I was
sitting at the window, staring at the sunset. I'm very
impressionable, I don't think, I feel things. I was lost in the
waves of golden light. Then a crowd came down the street with
children dancing before it. Women looked out of the windows.
They were carrying him past in a basket. The light shone on
his pale face, his curls were damp. He'd drowned himself. I
cried. All of me wept with a terrible longing. Then it was over.
Other people have weekdays and Sundays, they work six
days and pray on the seventh, they celebrate their birthdays,
they make New Year's resolutions. That way of living means
nothing to me. My life has no beginnings, no endings. All I
know is an endless longing and grasping, an endless fire, an
endless river. My mother died of grief because of me, people
point their fingers at me.

They're stupid. Only one thing matters, what gives you
pleasure? It may be bodies, pictures of Jesus, flowers, children's
toys. It's all the same. The more pleasure you get from life,
the more you say your prayers.

DANTON. Why can I never quite hold your beauty, never entirely
embrace you?

MARION. Danton, your lips have eyes.

DANTON. I'd like to be part of the ether so I could bathe you and flow over you, and break against every wave of your body.

Enter LACROIX, ADELAIDE *and* ROSALIE.

LACROIX (*remaining by the door*). I've got to laugh, I have got to laugh.

DANTON (*irritated*). At what?

LACROIX. In the street.

DANTON. Well?

LACROIX. I saw some dogs, a mastiff and a Bolognese lap-dog, getting up each other.

DANTON. And?

LACROIX. It made me laugh. An edifying spectacle. The girls were peering out of the windows, giggling. Young girls should not be allowed to sit in the sun or the gnats will be doing it in the palms of their hands, giving them ideas.

Well! Legendre and I have been through every cell of a holy place. The Little Nuns of The Word Made Flesh tore at our trousers begging for a benediction. Legendre is scourging one of them now. He'll get a month's fasting for that. And I bring with me two of the priestesses of the sacred body.

MARION. Good evening, demoiselle Adelaide, good evening demoiselle Rosalie.

ROSALIE. So long since we had the pleasure.

MARION. You should come and see us more often.

ADELAIDE. God! We don't stop day or night.

DANTON (*to* ROSALIE). Hey, little girl, your hips have grown deliciously.

ROSALIE. One tries to improve oneself.

LACROIX. What is the difference between the classical and the modern Adonis?

DANTON. And Adelaide, you look alluringly chaste. A piquant

variation. Her face looks like a fig-leaf that she holds in front
of her whole body. A fig-tree over a busy street, giving a pleasant
shade.

ADELAIDE. I'd be a cattle track if Monsieur —

DANTON. Point taken. But don't be spiteful, Mademoiselle.

LACROIX. No, listen. A modern Adonis isn't wounded in his
thigh, he's wounded in his private parts. And it's not roses
that spring from his blood, it's flowers of mercury.

DANTON. Mademoiselle Rosalie is a torso from a broken sculpture.
Restored. Only the hips and feet are from the original. She
is a magnetic needle: the North Pole repels, the South Pole
attracts. And in the middle is an equator, everyone who
crosses that line gets thrown in a bath of mercury.

LACROIX. Two sisters of mercy. Each works in a hospital; her
own body.

ROSALIE. Shame on you, you're making us blush.

ADELAIDE. Gentlemen, manners please.

ADELAIDE *and* ROSALIE *go off.*

DANTON. Goodnight, pretty children!

LACROIX. Goodnight, mines of mercury!

DANTON. I'm sorry for them, they only came for their supper.

LACROIX. Danton, listen. I've come from the Jacobins.

DANTON. No more news?

LACROIX. The people of Lyons have made a proclamation. The
gist of it — they despair and pull their togas about them, their
daggers are drawn and they are ready for suicide. Legendre
shouted out that people want to tear down the statues of
Marat and Chalier. I think he wants to smear some blood on
his face. Now he's survived the terror and children tug at his
coat in the street, he feels it's safe to pose as a revolutionary
monster.

DANTON. And Robespierre?

LACROIX. Pounced on the tribunal and said 'Virtue must rule

by terror'. Just the words gave me a pain in the neck.

DANTON. They plane planks for the guillotine.

LACROIX. And Collot shouted like a madman 'tear off the masks'.

DANTON. Do that and the faces will come off with them.

PARIS *comes on.*

LACROIX. What's happening, Fabricus?

PARIS. I went from the Jacobins straight to Robespierre. I demanded an explanation. He put on the expression of Brutus sacrificing his sons. He ranted about 'duty', said where liberty was concerned he was ruthless, he'd sacrifice everything, himself, his brothers, his friends.

DANTON. There you have it. One twist in the situation and he'll be holding the basket for the heads of his friends. We should thank Legendre for making him speak out.

LACROIX. I don't know. The Hébertists aren't quite dead yet. The deprivation amongst the people is overwhelming. Their suffering is a terrible lever.

If the pan of blood on the pair of scales lightens, it will swing up and become a lantern, to hang the Committee of Public Safety. Robespierre is after ballast: he needs one heavy head.

DANTON. The Revolution is like Saturn: it devours its own children. (*After some thought.*) No! They will not dare.

LACROIX. Danton, you are a dead saint of the Revolution. But the Revolution allows no relics, it has thrown the bones of all the kings into the street and all the statues out of the churches. Do you think they'll let you be a monument?

DANTON. My name! The people!

LACROIX. Your name! You're a moderate. So am I, so is Camille, Philippeau and Hérault. The people see moderation and weakness as one. They kill any stragglers. If those tailors of the red bonnet find the man of September to be a moderate compared to them, they'll cut the whole of Roman history to bits with their scissors.

DANTON. True, true. And the people are like children, they smash everything to see what's inside.

LACROIX. And Danton, we are what Robespierre says we are, we're true libertines, we enjoy life; but the people are virtuous, they don't enjoy life at all, work dulls them, all their organs of pleasure are clogged-up with dullness; they don't get drunk because they're broke, they don't go to brothels because their breath stinks of cheese and herrings and disgusts the girls.

DANTON. They hate pleasure seekers like a eunuch hates men.

LACROIX. We get called scoundrels and (*speaking into* DANTON's *ear*:) between ourselves, there's a half-truth there. Robespierre and the people *are* virtuous. St. Just will write a philosophical treatise on it and Barère, Barère will tailor a red jacket and a speech to clothe the Convention in blood and — I see it all.

DANTON. You're dreaming! They never had courage without me. Now they'll never have courage to move against me. The Revolution isn't done yet. They may need me again. They'll keep me in their arsenal.

LACROIX. We must act. Now.

DANTON. It'll come right in the end.

LACROIX. We'll all be dead before then.

MARION (*to* DANTON). Your lips have gone cold. Words have choked your kisses.

DANTON (*to* MARION). So many words, so much time to wade through. Is it worth it? (*To* LACROIX.) Tomorrow, I'll go and see Robespierre. I'll provoke him so that he can't remain silent. Tomorrow then! Goodnight my friends, goodnight, goodnight, I thank you.

LACROIX. Come then gentlemen. Goodnight Danton. The lady's thighs will guillotine you, the mound of Venus will be your Tarpeian Rock.

He goes off, with PARIS.

Scene Six

A room.

ROBESPIERRE, DANTON, PARIS.

ROBESPIERRE. I say to you, he who stays my arm when I draw my sword is my enemy. His motives are irrelevant. He who stops me defending myself kills me as surely as if he attacked me.

DANTON. Where self-defence ends, murder begins. I see no reason that compels us to go on killing.

ROBESPIERRE. The social revolution is not yet over. He who makes only half a revolution digs his own grave. The old ruling class is not yet dead. The healthy vigour of the people must utterly usurp the place of that class, which has frittered itself away. Vice must be punished, virtue must rule through terror.

DANTON. I do not understand the word 'punishment'. You and your virtue, Robespierre! You take no bribes, run up no debts, sleep with no women, always wear a clean coat and never get drunk. Robespierre, you are abominably virtuous. I'd be disgusted if I'd spent thirty years with such a self-righteous expression stuck on my face, running about between heaven and earth, only for the miserable pleasure of finding people worse than myself. Is there nothing in you, not the merest whisper, that says to you, very softly and very secretly, 'You lie! You lie!'

ROBESPIERRE. My conscience is clear.

DANTON. Conscience is an ape tormenting himself before a mirror. We all dress ourselves up in high morals, then go on the town to get the good time we want. Why get in each other's hair about it? I say, each man to his own pleasure; and the right to defend himself against anyone who threatens it. But you! Have you the right to turn the guillotine into a tub, to wash people's dirty laundry with their severed heads for scouring stones, and all because you like to wear a clean coat? Yes, if they spit on it or tear holes in it, defend yourself, but what business is it of yours as long as they leave you in peace? If they're happy going about in dirty clothes, does that give you the right to slam them into their graves? Are you the policeman of heaven? If you and your Supreme Being don't like it, hold a handkerchief to your nose.

ROBESPIERRE. Do you deny virtue?

DANTON. And vice. There are only Epicureans, some fine, some gross. Christ was the finest of all. That is the only distinction I draw between men. Each acts according to his nature, that is — do what does you good. Eh, Incorruptible! A shock is it, to have your high-heels kicked from under you?

ROBESPIERRE. Danton, at certain times vice is high treason.

DANTON. Oh no, don't ban it, don't proscribe it. You are in its debt. Purity needs vice, if only for the contrast. To use your terminology, our blows must profit the Republic. We must never strike down the innocent along with the guilty.

ROBESPIERRE. Who tells you one innocent man has died?

DANTON. You hear that, Fabricus? No innocent man has died. (*He goes off, addressing* PARIS *as he leaves.*) We must move, now! We must declare ourselves.

DANTON *and* PARIS *go off.*

ROBESPIERRE (*alone*). Go then. Like a coachman with a team of broken hacks, he wants the fiery steeds of the revolution to stop at the nearest brothel. But they'll bolt and have strength enough to drag him to the Place de la Revolution.

Kick my high heels? Use my terminology? Mine?

No. Stop. Is that what they will say? That his gigantic bulk cast a shadow over me and that is why I sent him out of the sun? For personal spite?

Would they be right?

Is it necessary? Yes! Yes! The Republic! He must go.

My thoughts watch each other. He must go. He who stands still in a crowd that presses forward, in effect moves in resistance against it, and he will be trampled underfoot.

We will not let the ship of the Revolution run aground on the
shallow calculations, the mudbanks of these people; we must
cut off the hand of anyone who holds it back. Down with
a society that destroys aristocrats only to put on their clothes
and inherit their sores.

No virtue? Virtue the heel of my shoe? My terminology?
Thought against thought, why can't I stop?

Something inside me. A bloody finger, pointing. I wind
rags around it but the blood seeps through.

A pause.

There. There. Inside me, telling lies to all the rest of me.

He goes to the window.

Night snores over the earth and shifts in a desolate dream.
Insubstantial thoughts, desires only dimly suspected,
confused, formless, take shape and steal into the silent house
of dreams. They open the doors, stare out of the windows,
they become half-flesh, the limbs stretch the lips move. And
when we wake, we may be brighter, more precise, more
concrete by daylight, but are we not still in a dream? Oh what
the mind does, who can blame us? The mind goes through
more actions in one hour than the lumbering body does in a
lifetime. A thought may be a sin, but whether or not that
thought becomes a deed, whether the body acts upon it, is
chance. Chance.

ST JUST *comes on.*

Who's that in the dark? Light! Light!

ST JUST. Don't you know my voice?

ROBESPIERRE. Ah. You, St Just.

A SERVANT GIRL *brings a light.*

ST JUST. Were you alone?

ROBESPIERRE. Danton's just left.

ST JUST. I saw him in the Palais Royal. He was wearing his
revolutionary face and coining epigrams. He was on christian

names with the Sans-culottes, the tarts were running at his heels, the crowd hung about whispering every word he said. We'll lose the initiative. Why do you hesitate? We will act without you. We are resolved.

ROBESPIERRE. What will you do?

ST JUST. We are summoning the Committees, Legislative, General Security and Public Safety, to a full session.

ROBESPIERRE. A grand affair.

ST JUST. We will bury the great corpse with dignity, like priests, not assassins. We will not hack at it, it will go down, whole.

ROBESPIERRE. Be plain.

ST JUST. We must lay him to rest in full armour. Slaughter his horses and his slaves on his burial mound. Lacroix —

ROBESPIERRE. An outright criminal. Former lawyer's clerk, now Lieutenant-General of France. Go on.

ST JUST. Hérault-Séchelles.

ROBESPIERRE. A handsome head.

ST JUST. He was the beautifully illuminated initial letter of the Act of the Constitution. We no longer need ornamental flourishes. He will be effaced. Philippeau, Camille —

ROBESPIERRE. Camille?

ST JUST (*hands him a paper*). I thought you would be startled. Read that.

ROBESPIERRE. 'Le Vieux Cordelier'? Is that all? Childish satire. Camille just made fun of you —

ST JUST. Read, here! Here! (*He indicates a place.*)

ROBESPIERRE (*reads*). 'This Messiah of blood, Robespierre, this Christ in reverse, stands on his Calvary between the two thieves Cothon and Collot. He is not sacrificed, he sacrifices. The devout sisters of the guillotine stand below like Mary and Magdelene. St Just, like St John the Evangelist, is at his bosom and delivers the apocalyptic revelations of the Master to the Convention: he holds up his head as if it were the sacrament itself.'

ST JUST. I'll make him hold up his in a basket.

ROBESPIERRE (*reads on*). 'The clean frock coat of the Messiah is France's winding sheet, his fingers rapping on the tribunal are the blades of the guillotine. And you, Barère, who said that coins, not heads, would be struck in the Place de la Revolution — but no I won't upset that old hag. Why is he an old hag? Because he is like a widow who has driven half a dozen husbands to their graves. That is his talent, people he smiles upon have a habit of dying six months later. What can one do for a man who sits by the corpses of his friends to enjoy the stink?'

Oh Camille, you too?

Down with them! Now! Only the dead are harmless. Have you got the indictment ready?

ST JUST. It's quickly done. You said it all at the Jacobin Club.

ROBESPIERRE. I wanted to frighten them.

ST JUST. I'll elaborate a little. A meal of accusations. They'll choke to death on it, I give you my word.

ROBESPIERRE. And tomorrow, quickly! No long death agony! These past few days I've become — sensitive. Just be quick!

ST JUST *goes off.*

Messiah of blood, who is not sacrificed but sacrifices. Yes. He redeemed them with his blood. I redeem them with their own. He made them sinners, I take the sin upon me. He had the ecstasy of pain. I have the torment of the executioner. Who denies himself the more, he or I?

Foolish. The thoughts. Foolish.

Why do we always look at that man? The son of man is crucified in all of us, we all agonise in a bloody sweat, each in our own Gethsemane, but no one man redeems another by his wounds. Oh my Camille! They all go from me. The night is bleak and empty. I am alone.

Act Two

Scene One

A room.

DANTON, LACROIX, PHILIPPEAU, PARIS, CAMILLE DESMOULINS.

CAMILLE. Quick, Danton. We're losing time.

DANTON (*he is dressing himself*). I think time is losing us. You put on your shirt, then your trousers over it, you crawl into bed at night and out in the morning, you put one foot in front of the other. Sad. There is absolutely no vision of any other way of doing it: millions have always done it like that, millions always will. And since we're split into two halves, two arms and two legs, everything's done twice. It's all very boring and very, very sad.

CAMILLE. You are talking childishly.

DANTON. Dying men are often childish.

LACROIX. By delaying you rush headlong towards ruin, dragging all your friends with you. Rally the cowards to you, from all the parties, plain and mountain. Cry out against the tyranny of the Decemvirs. Speak of daggers, Brutus, frighten Robespierre's tribunes, use anyone, even what's left of the Hébertists. Give vent to your anger! Don't let us die disarmed and humiliated like the wretched Hébert.

DANTON. Don't you remember you called me a dead saint? You were nearer the truth than you knew. I was with the Sans-culottes. They were full of respect but like a crowd at a funeral. You were right, I'm a relic and relics are thrown onto the street.

LACROIX. Why did you let it come to this?

DANTON. Come to this? I got bored. Bored, going round
wearing the same coat, pulling the same face. Contemptible.
A pathetic instrument with one string, one note. I just
couldn't go on, I wanted a rest. Well, I've got it. The
Revolution is offering me retirement, though rather
differently than I imagined. Besides, who supports me?
Our whores may be a match for the nuns of the guillotine,
but that's all. You can count it on the fingers of one hand:
the Jacobin Club has declared virtue the order of the day,
the Cordelier Club call me Hébert's executioner, the
Commune is doing penance, and the Convention — well, we
could try to win there, but it would be the 31st. of May all
over again. They won't give in easily: Robespierre is the
dogma of the Revolution, it cannot be denied. No, it won't
work. I would rather be guillotined, than guillotine. I no
longer understand why we fight each other, we should sit
down and have peace. We were botched when we were
created, we lack something, some element. I can't name it,
but we won't find it by pulling each other's guts out and
scrabbling around in each other's entrails. Bah — we are
pitiful alchemists.

CAMILLE. Translated into the grand, tragic style that would
go like this: how long must mankind eat its own limbs in
eternal hunger? Or: how long must we men, marooned on a
wreck, suck each others blood in unquenchable thirst? Or:
how long must we algebraists of the flesh, hunting for the
ever elusive and unknown x write out equations in mangled
limbs?

DANTON. You're a strong echo.

CAMILLE. Yes aren't I. You fire the pistol, I come back like a
peal of thunder. All the better for you, you should keep me
with you.

PHILIPPEAU. So France is left with its executioners?

DANTON. People do very well, the way things are. They're
oppressed, but at least they're not bored. They can
be noble, fine-feeling, virtuous, witty, what more do they
want? What's it matter if you die by guillotine, or by fever or

old age? Better to be young and supple, as you stride to the
wings saying your last lines on earth. The audience applauds
and we all love it! It's all gesture, all acting, even if you do
get really stabbed to death at the end. Excellent thing,
to shorten life a little. It's a coat that's far too long, anyway.
Good! Let life be an epigram, excellent, who has breath and
spirit to slog their way through an epic poem of fifty or sixty
cantos? Better a sip of spirits from a tiny glass, than a tub of
undrinkable beer. And, above all — I'd have to shout. The
effort is too great. Life is not worth all the sweat and strain
needed, merely to preserve it.

PARIS. Then run, Danton, get away!

DANTON. Can you take your country with you on the soles of
your shoes? And anyway, when it comes down to it: they
will not dare. (*To* CAMILLE.) Come on, my boy. I tell you,
they will not dare! So, adieu! Adieu!

DANTON *and* CAMILLE *go off.*

PHILIPPEAU. And off he goes.

LACROIX. Not believing a word he says. It's sheer laziness!
He'd let himself be guillotined because he can't be bothered
to make a speech.

PARIS. What do we do now?

LACROIX. Go home, like Lucrece, and prepare to die
gracefully.

Scene Two

A promenade: WALKERS.

CITIZEN. My dear Teresa, sorry I mean Corn, Cor —

SIMON. Cornelia, citizen, Cornelia.

CITIZEN. Cornelia. She's blessed me with a baby boy!

SIMON. Wrong! Has borne the Republic a son.

CITIZEN. Yes, has — to the Republic. But isn't that a bit general? I don't want people to think —

SIMON. No. The particular must yield to the general.

CITIZEN. Yes. That's what my wife says.

BALLAD SINGER. What then oh then
                Do men desire
                Where then oh then
                Is pleasure's fire?

CITIZEN. I'm a bit stuck on names.

SIMON. Christen him Pike.

CITIZEN. Pike?

SIMON. As in 'head on a . . .' Second name, Marat.

CITIZEN. Pike Marat. Ah.

BALLAD SINGER. Why then oh then
                Are cares so long
                Why then oh then
                Are days so long?

CITIZEN. I'd like three names. There's something about the number three. Really, the first name should be something practical and the second name something political. Why not the first name Plough and second name Robespierre — and the third —

SIMON. Pike!

CITIZEN. Plough Robespierre Pike. Good names for a boy, a good start in life. Thank you, citizen.

SIMON. May Cornelia's breast be the udder of the Roman she-wolf! Oh. No, that won't do, Romulus was a tyrant, that won't do at all. May —

They pass on.

A BEGGAR (*sings*). Life is no loss
                     Toss the dice
                     What do you win?

A handful of earth
A little moss —
Kind sirs, pretty ladies —

1ST GENTLEMAN. Get back to work! You look well enough fed.

2ND GENTLEMAN. Here! (*He gives him money*.) Hand with a
skin like velvet. It's scandalous.

BEGGAR. Sir, how did you get that coat?

2ND GENTLEMAN. By work, work! If you want some, come
and see me. I live —

BEGGAR. Sir, why did you work?

2ND GENTLEMAN. To get the coat, you fool.

BEGGAR. But that coat is a pleasure, when a rag will do, so you
worked for pleasure.

2ND GENTLEMAN. Of course I did! That's the system.

BEGGAR. And he calls me a fool. The two things cancel each
other out. Meanwhile the sun's warm in the street and
life is there to be lived.

(*sings*). A handful of earth
A little moss —
Kind . . .

He passes on.

ROSALIE (*to* ADELAIDE). Come on! Soldiers. And we've not had
anything hot in us all day.

SOLDIER. Halt, and all that! And where are you going, little
girls? (*To* ROSALIE.) I say, how old are you?

ROSALIE. As old as my little finger.

SOLDIER. Oh, very sharp.

ROSALIE. And you are very blunt.

SOLDIER. Then I'll sharpen myself on you.

(*Sings*).   Am I hurting ya, Christina?
Do ya want 'a shed a tear?
Am I hurting ya, Christina
Do you feel me right in 'ere?

SOLDIER. Supper?

DANTON *and* CAMILLE *come on.*

DANTON. Isn't it jolly? I smell it in the air. A scent, a musk. The sun is hatching out lechery. Doesn't it make you want to tear your trousers off and hump them all, like dogs in the street?

They pass on.

YOUNG GENTLEMAN. Madame. The peel of a bell, the evening light on the trees, the first stars.

MADAME. Yes, the perfume of the flowers, the purity of nature. (*To* EUGENIE.) You see, Eugenie, virtue sees the pleasures of nature, and smiles.

EUGENIE (*kisses her* MOTHER's *hands*). Mama, I only see you.

MADAME. Dear child.

YOUNG GENTLEMAN (*whispering in* EUGENIE's *ear*). You see that pretty woman with that old man?

EUGENIE. I know her.

YOUNG GENTLEMAN. They say her hairdresser has styled her in the family way.

EUGENIE (*laughs*). That's wicked gossip.

YOUNG GENTLEMAN. No. The old man sees the bud swelling and takes her for a walk in the sun, thinking he's the thunderstorm that watered it.

EUGENIE. Don't be crude, you'll make me blush.

YOUNG GENTLEMAN. Do that and you'll make me go pale.

They go off.

DANTON (*to* CAMILLE). Don't! Don't expect anything serious from me. I can't see why people don't just stand still in the street and laugh in each other's face. We should all laugh. From our windows, from our graves, 'til heaven bursts open and the earth spins with laughter.

They go off.

1ST GENTLEMAN. I am telling you, it is a major discovery. It will turn science on its head. Humanity strides toward its great destiny.

2ND GENTLEMAN. Did you see that new play? The hanging gardens of Babylon! A maze of vaults, stairways, corridors, flung up into the air with extraordinary ease. Outrageous audacity, it gives you vertigo. An amazing mind.

He stands still, at a loss.

Give me your hand.

1ST GENTLEMAN. What's wrong?

2ND GENTLEMAN. There. That puddle. It could have been deep.

1ST GENTLEMAN. The puddle frightened you . . .

2ND GENTLEMAN. Forgive me. The earth has a thin crust. You could fall through a hole in the middle of the street. One must tread carefully. But as for the play, I recommend it.

Scene Three

A room.

DANTON, CAMILLE, LUCILE.

CAMILLE. I tell you, if they don't get everything in wooden reproductions, in their theatres, concerts, art exhibitions, they won't even listen. But if they get a ridiculous marionette and they can see the strings moving it up and down and they can see its legs creaking along in iambic pentameters, they say 'What truth! What understanding of human nature, how profound!' Take any tiny insight, any fatuous notion or tin-pot aphorism, dress it up, and paint it in bright colours and parade it about for three acts 'til it gets married or shoots itself, and they cry 'What idealism!' If someone grinds out an opera which echoes the ebb and flow of human experience about as well as a clay pipe echoes a nightingale: 'Such artistry!' But turn them out of the theatre into the street and,

oh dear, reality is just too sordid. They forget God himself,
they prefer his bad imitators. Creation is being newly born
every minute, within them and all around them, glowing, a
storm glittering with lightning: but they hear and see nothing.
They go to the theatre, read poems and novels and praise the
caricatures. To creation itself they say "How ugly, how boring'.

The Greeks warned us about literature with the story of
Pygmalion's statue, the stone come to life but unable to
bear children.

DANTON. And artists treat nature like David. When the
massacred of September were thrown out of La Force Prison
onto the street, he stood there cold-bloodedly drawing
them. He said 'I'm capturing the last twitches of life in these
bastards'.

DANTON *is called outside.*

CAMILLE. What do you say, Lucile?

LUCILE. I just love to watch you talk.

CAMILLE. But do you hear what I say?

LUCILE. Of course.

CAMILLE. But am I right? Did you really hear what I said?

LUCILE. Well, no. Not really.

DANTON *returns.*

CAMILLE. What's wrong?

DANTON. The Committee of Public Safety has decided to
arrest me. Someone's warned me and offered me a place to hide.
They want my head? Let them have it. I'm sick of this rigmarole.
What's it matter? I'll know how to die with courage, it'll be
easier than living.

CAMILLE. Danton, there's still time . . .

DANTON. No, no. But I never thought they'd —

CAMILLE. Danton, your laziness!

DANTON. I'm not lazy, just tired. But! It's getting too hot
for me here.

CAMILLE. Where you going?

DANTON. Guess.

CAMILLE. Seriously, where?

DANTON. A walk, my boy. I'm going for a walk.

DANTON *goes off.*

LUCILE. Camille!

CAMILLE. Don't worry, my love.

LUCILE. When I think what they might do with this head.
Camille, that's nonsense, isn't it?

CAMILLE. Don't worry. I'm no Danton.

LUCILE. The world's so rich, so big, so full of things. And full
of so many men's heads. Why this one, who's got the right to
take this one away from me? It's too cruel. What do they
want with it?

CAMILLE. I told you, there's no need to worry. I spoke to
Robespierre, yesterday. He was very friendly. It's true we're a
little estranged, but we have different ways of looking at
things, that's all.

LUCILE. Go and see him.

CAMILLE. We sat on the same bench at school. He was always
moody and lonely. I was the only one who sought him out
and made him laugh. He's always been very fond of me. I'll
go now.

LUCILE. Now, my friend? Go. No, come here. This — (*She
kisses him.*) and this! Go! Go!

CAMILLE *goes off.*

A cruel time. That is how things are. What can we do? We
must just keep quiet.

(*Sings*). Ah parting, parting and sorrow
         Who thought love would end —

A song? In my head? It's not good it should just spring up
like that. He turned away, I thought 'I'll never see him walk

back'. He'll go further and further away. The room is so
empty. The windows are open as if there's a corpse laid out
in here. I can't bear it.

She goes off.

Scene Four

Open country.

DANTON. I won't go on, disturbing the silence, feet scuffing,
lungs panting.

He sits down. A pause.

Someone told me, once, there's an illness that makes you
lose your memory. Death must be like that. I hope he'll do
more, and wipe out everything. I hope he will. My memories
are my enemies. I'd turn my cheek, like a good Christian, and
offer them salvation gladly. It safe here in the country? Huh.
Safe enough for memories, but not for me. My only safety
is in the grave. That is my only guarantee for the obliteration
of memory. But, back there, in people's minds, 'my memory'
is still alive. It is kicking me to death. Me or it? The answer's
simple.

He stands and turns back.

A flirtation with death! It's rather amusing, ogling him from a
distance through my lorgnette. This business makes me laugh.
A sense of permanence tells me — there'll be a tomorrow
after today, a day after tomorrow, everything as it was.
Empty threats! They only want to frighten me. They will not
dare.

Scene Five

A room. Night time.

DANTON (*at the window*). Will it never stop? Will the light never die, the noise never stop? Will it never be dark and silent so we can stop hearing our foul sins? September!

JULIE (*calls from within*). Danton! Danton!

DANTON. Eh?

JULIE (*enters*). What were you shouting?

DANTON. Did I shout?

JULIE. 'Foul sins', you said. Then you shouted, 'September'.

DANTON. Me? No, didn't say anything. They were faint, private thoughts.

JULIE. You're trembling, Danton.

DANTON. Trembling? What do you expect when the walls begin to speak, when your body breaks apart and thoughts wander off and speak from bricks and stones? It's not good.

JULIE. Georges, my Georges —

DANTON. Not good. Stop thinking altogether if thought's going to turn straight into speech. There are some thoughts, Julie, that must never, ever be heard. It's not good if they cry out the second they're born, like a baby from the womb. Not good.

JULIE. God preserve your reason, Georges. Georges do you know who I am?

DANTON. A human being, a woman, my wife. And the world has five continents. Europe, Asia, Africa, America, Australia, two and two are four. Reason intact. You say I shouted September?

JULIE. Yes, Danton. I heard it right through the house.

DANTON. I went to the window and — (*He looks out.*) The city's quiet, the lights are out —

JULIE. There's a child crying, somewhere near.

DANTON. I went to the window and there was a cry of outrage
in every street, September!

JULIE. You were dreaming, Danton, calm yourself.

DANTON. Dreaming. But there was something else. My head's
swimming, wait. There! I remember. The earth's globe
was panting as it span, in space. My limbs were gigantic, I
pounced on the globe and rode it bareback like a runaway
horse, I gripped its flanks with my legs, I clutched its mane,
my hair streamed above the abyss, I shouted in terror: and
woke. Then I got up, went to the window and heard that
word, Julie. Why that word? What does that word want of
me, why does it reach out its bloody hands?

My mind's numb. Julie, wasn't it September when —

JULIE. The monarchs were only forty hours from Paris —

DANTON. The fortresses had fallen. The aristocrats were in the
city —

JULIE. The Republic was lost.

DANTON. Lost. We couldn't leave the enemy at our backs, we'd
have been fools. Two enemies on a plank. Them or us. The
stronger throws the other off. Fair? Fair, no?

JULIE. Yes, yes.

DANTON. It wasn't murder, it was civil war.

JULIE. You saved your country.

DANTON. I did, I did. We had to do it, it was self-defence. The
man on the cross took the easy way out: 'It is impossible but
that offences will come: but woe unto him through whom
they come.'

Impossible, but it was necessary. Who can curse the hand on
which the curse of necessity falls? But who says it was
necessary? What is it in us that whores, lies, steals, murders?

We are puppets of unknown forces. We ourselves are nothing,
nothing! We are the swords with which invisible spirits fight —
and we can't even see their hands.

I feel calmer now.

JULIE. Quite calm, my dear?

DANTON. Yes, Julie. Come to bed.

Scene Six

A street in front of DANTON's *house.*

SIMON, CITIZEN-SOLDIERS.

SIMON. How advances the night?

CITIZEN. How does the night what?

SIMON. How does the night advance?

CITIZEN. It gets dark, stays dark, then gets light again.

SIMON. Fool! What's the time?

CITIZEN. The time when the pendulums of men, swing under the sheets.

SIMON. Silence, all of you! Danton's house. In we go! Forward Citizens! Dead or alive! Beware, he is a powerful brute. I'll lead the way, citizens. Clear the way for liberty! Look to my wife. She'll cock a crown of oak leaves on her head.

1ST CITIZEN. A crown of cocks? I do hear she likes the odd acorn falling in her lap.

SIMON. On citizens, your country will be grateful.

2ND CITIZEN. I wish I could be grateful back. For all the holes we make in people's bodies, there's not one less hole in our trousers.

1ST CITIZEN. Want your flies sewn up then? (*He laughs.*)

SIMON. Forward!

They force a way into DANTON's *house.*

Scene Seven

A group of DEPUTIES.

LEGENDRE. Is the butchery of deputies to go on? Who will be
    safe if Danton falls?

1ST DEPUTY. What can we do?

2ND DEPUTY. He must be tried by the Convention. Success will
    be ours. Nothing can drown that voice.

3RD DEPUTY. Impossible. A decree prevents it.

LEGENDRE. Repeal it. Make an exception. I'll put the motion.
    I rely on your support.

PRESIDENT. The session is open.

LEGENDRE (*ascends the tribunal*). Last night four members of
    the National Convention were arrested. Danton is one of
    them. The names of the others I do not know. But I demand
    they be tried before the Assembly. Citizens! I hold Danton to
    be as spotless as myself and I reproach myself with nothing. I
    attack no member of the Committees of Public Safety or
    General Security, but I fear there are personal feuds, private
    hatreds that may rob Liberty of men who gave her great
    service. The man who by his energy, his passion saved France
    in the year 1792 deserves a hearing. If he, indeed, is to stand
    accused of high treason, give him the right to defend himself.

    Violent commotion.

A FEW VOICES. We support Legendre's motion.

1ST DEPUTY. The people put us here. Only our electors can
    get rid of us.

2ND DEPUTY. Your words smell of corpses! Words out of the
    mouths of the Girondins! No privileges! Only the axe of
    justice over every head!

3RD DEPUTY. Our Committees must not with-hold the
    sanctuary of the law from our legislators and send them to
    the guillotine!

4TH DEPUTY. Crime has no sanctuary! Only criminals in

crowns find sanctuary, on their thrones.

5TH DEPUTY. Only criminals ask for sanctuary.

6TH DEPUTY. Only assassins deny it.

ROBESPIERRE. Not for many a long day has this assembly been
thrown into such confusion. And no wonder: we have come
to a crisis. Today will decide whether a handful of men will,
or will not, defeat their country. How can you betray your
principles so far that, today, you will grant to a few individuals
what, yesterday, you denied Chabot, Delaunay and Fabre?
What is behind this favouritism to a few men? What do I care
for the eulogies people make about themselves and their
friends? We know their true worth. We do not ask if a man
did this or that patriotic act, we question his entire political
career. Legendre appears to be ignorant of the names of the
detainees. But the whole Convention knows them. Who is
amongst them? His friend Lacroix. Why does Legendre appear
not to know that? Because he knows all too well only a cynic
could defend Lacroix. He names Danton because he thinks a
privilege is attached to that name. We want no privileges, we
want no false gods!

Applause.

What sets Danton above Lafayette or Dumouriez, Brissot,
Fabre, Chabot, Hébert? What did we say about them that we
cannot say about him? Did you spare them? What has he
done to deserve privileges above his fellow citizens? Could it
be that a few deluded men, and others less deluded, banded
together to seek power and fortune with him in his retinue?
The greater, then, his betrayal of patriots who put their trust
in him, the more severely must he feel the wrath of lovers
of liberty.

They want to fill you with fear of an abuse of power. The
power that you yourselves wield. They cry out against the
despotism of the Committees. But you bring the trust of the
people to the Committees, that trust is an absolute protection
for true patriots. They present themselves as trembling with
fear. But I say to you, he who trembles at this moment is
guilty, for innocence never trembles before public vigilance.

General applause.

They tried to scare me too. They wrote to me. They warned
me that I am surrounded by Danton's friends, that the danger
he faces could, in turn, come to me. With these threats
cloaked in simulated virtues and appeals to old loyalties, they
tried to moderate my zeal and passion for liberty. So I now
declare: nothing will restrain me, not even if Danton's
danger becomes my own. All of us need a degree of courage
and greatness of spirit. Only criminals and the spiritually
crippled are afraid to see their kind fall by their side. For, when
they are no longer hidden by a crowd of accomplices, they
find themselves naked and exposed in the harsh light of truth.
But if there are spiritual cripples in this assembly, there are
also heroes. The number of criminals is not that great. We need
only strike a few heads and the country is saved.

Applause.

I demand that Legendre's motion be rejected.

The DEPUTIES *rise as a body to indicate their unanimous
agreement.*

ST JUST. It seems there are, in this assembly, a few sensitive
ears that cannot stand the word 'blood'. A few general
observations will show them that we are no more cruel than
nature or the age we live in. Nature obeys her laws calmly and
inexorably. If man comes into conflict with them he is
destroyed. A change in the constituent parts of the air, a
flare-up of subterranean fires, a fluctuation in the water level,
a plague, a volcanic eruption, a flood, these send thousands
to their graves. But what is the final reckoning? An
insignificant, almost imperceptible change in physical nature,
which would almost leave no trace, but for the corpses which
lie in its wake.

So I ask you now: should the moral nature be more cautious
than the physical nature about *its* revolutions? Should not an
idea, just like a law of physics, be allowed to destroy what
opposes it? Why should an event that transforms the whole
of humanity not advance through blood? The world spirit

employs the hand with a sword in the spiritual sphere, just as he employs volcanoes or floods in the physical. What is the difference between death by pestilence and death by revolution?

Mankind advances slowly. Its steps can only be counted centuries later. Behind each footprint rise the graves of generations. The achievement of the simplest inventions and principles cost the lives of millions. Is it not to be expected that now, when history speeds faster than ever before, many men will fall, their last breath spent?

We close with a simple point. We were all created in the same way. But for the minor variations made by nature herself, we are all equal. Therefore, everyone is superior and no one is privileged, neither an individual or a smaller or larger class of individuals. And every clause of that sentence, when put into practice, has killed its men! The 14th of July, 10th of August and the 31st of May are its punctuation marks. The physical world would take centuries to do what we have done, punctuated by generations. We took four years. Is it, then, so surprising that at every turn of the tide the great sea of the Revolution washes up its corpses?

We still have a few clauses to complete our sentence. Are a few more corpses going to stop us? Moses led his people across the Red Sea and let the old, corrupt generation die out before he founded his new state. We do not have the Red Sea or the desert, we have war and the guillotine.

Like Pelias's daughters, the Revolution cuts up mankind to rejuvanate it. Humanity will emerge from the bloodbath like the world after the flood, restored, newly created.

Long drawn out applause.

All you secret enemies of tyranny, in Europe, in the whole world, who carry Brutus's dagger under your robes, come! Join us at this sublime moment.

The DEPUTIES *and* OTHERS *strike up the 'Marseillaise'.*

Act Three

Scene One

The Luxembourg. A room containing PRISONERS.
CHAUMETTE, PAINE, HÉRAULT DE SÉCHELLES,
MERCIER *and other* PRISONERS.

CHAUMETTE (*tugs at* PAINE's *sleeve*). Listen, Paine. You
convinced me yesterday but today I've got a headache. I'm
depressed. Cheer me up with your syllogisms.

PAINE. Right then, Anaxagoras the Philosopher: your
catechism. Here we go. There is no God. For: God created
the world or he did not. If he did not, then the world
contains its own origins and there is no God, since God is
only God because he contains all origins of all being. And
again: God cannot have created the world, for creation is
either eternal, like God, or it had a beginning. If it did have a
beginning, God must have created it at a specific moment in
time. That is: God must have been passive for an eternity,
then upped and begun. That is, changed from passive to
active, and begun history itself, that is time. But 'time' and
'change' are concepts incompatible with God who is
endlessly eternal and endlessly himself. Therefore, God
cannot have created the world. But since we all know the
world exists, or at least that we exist, and since from the
foregoing argument the world has its origins in itself or in
something not God, there is no God. *Quod erat
demonstrandum.*

CHAUMETTE. Ah. Yes. Daylight again. Thank you, thank you.

MERCIER. Hold on, Paine. What if creation is eternal?

PAINE. Then it is simply not creation, it is a part of God. As
Spinoza says, God is in everything, in your excellent self, in
the Philosopher Anaxagoras here and in me. That wouldn't

be so bad, except that if God is us and we our God, there's not much divine majesty for the Dear Lord if he can get toothache via anyone of us, or the clap.

MERCIER. But there must be a first cause.

PAINE. Undeniably. But who tells you the first cause is God, that is perfection? Do you think this world is perfect?

MERCIER. No.

PAINE. Then how can a perfect cause, cause an imperfect effect? I know Voltaire backslid on that one, but he no more dared argue against God than argue against kings. The man who has nothing but his reason, and does not or dare not deny God, is a bad workman.

MERCIER. Against that, let me ask this question. Can a perfect cause have a perfect effect? In other words, can something that is perfect create something perfect? Isn't that impossible, since a thing that is created cannot contain its own origins? As you said, that is an attribute of perfection.

CHAUMETTE. Oh stop it, stop it!

PAINE. Calm down, Philosopher, we will get there. You are right: but if you are going to say God creates but can only create something imperfect, then he'd be wiser not to start at all. Doesn't it strike you as a very human trait, that we can only imagine God as a creator? Because we are always up and doing, just to convince ourselves that we exist? We are always ascribing to God our own miserable urges! Why do we take it for granted that eternity is itching to flex its fingers and start making little bread men on the table? We whisper to ourselves it is out of overwhelming love. But do we need to get into all that to convince ourselves we are the sons of God? I'd rather have a lesser father. I'd not have to accuse him of bringing us up in pig-sties and slave galleys.

You can only prove the existence of God if you deny the world is imperfect. Spinoza tried it. You deny the existence of evil, but not pain. Only false reason can prove God. All true feelings rebel against it. Anaxagoras, why do I suffer? That is the rock of atheism. The slightest twinge of pain, even in a single atom, and creation is smashed, top to bottom.

MERCIER. And morality?

PAINE. First you use morality to prove God exists, then God to prove morality exists. Who needs morality? I don't know what is inherently good or inherently bad, so I ignore it. I act according to my nature, what is good for me I do, what is bad for me I don't do, and defend myself against when it comes for me. You can be what people call virtuous and defend yourself against what they call vice, without despising others who differ from you. To despise they who do not share your view of the world is deplorable.

CHAUMETTE. True, very true!

HÉRAULT. Ah, but, Philosopher Anaxagoras, it can be said that if God is everything, then he is also his own opposite, both perfect and imperfect, good and evil, pleasure and suffering. Ah, but then the answer would be 'nought', everything crossed out, we'd end up with nothing. Be content, you come out of the argument very well. With a clear conscience you can worship an actress on the stage playing the Goddess of reason, nature's masterpiece, and count the rosary of sores she gave you in her dressing room.

CHAUMETTE. I'm most obliged to you, Gentlemen.

He goes off.

PAINE. A man unsure. When all's said and argued, he'll take extreme unction, turn his toes to Mecca and have himself circumcised, just to be on the safe side.

DANTON, LACROIX, CAMILLE *and* PHILIPPEAU *are led in.*

HÉRAULT (*rushes to* DANTON *and embraces him*). Do I say good morning or goodnight? I won't ask if you've slept. How we'll ever sleep again, I don't know.

DANTON. Oh, by going to bed, laughing.

MERCIER. A bull mastiff with the wings of a dove. The evil genius of the Revolution. He tried to rape his mother but she was too strong for him.

PAINE. His life and his death are equal catastrophes.

LACROIX (*to* DANTON). I never thought they'd arrest us so quickly.

DANTON. I did, I was warned.

LACROIX. And you said nothing?

DANTON. Why say something? I'd rather die of a heart attack suddenly; why make it a long, long illness? (*To* HÉRAULT.) Better to lay down on the earth than get corns, trampling over it, eh? I prefer the earth as a cushion, rather than a hassock.

HÉRAULT. At least we won't have old men's leathery skin on our fingers when we stroke the cheeks of the lovely lady putrefaction.

CAMILLE. Don't bother, Danton, don't trouble yourself. Not now. No matter how far you stick out your tongue, you'll not lick the sweat of death off your forehead. Oh, Lucile, what a tragedy.

The PRISONERS *gather round the new arrivals.*

DANTON (*to* PAINE). What you did for the good of your country, I tried to do for mine. I've had less luck than you, they're sending me to the scaffold. Let them, I won't stumble.

MERCIER (*to* DANTON). The blood of the twenty-two is choking you.

1ST PRISONER (*to* HÉRAULT). The might of the people and the might of reason are one.

2ND PRISONER (*to* CAMILLE). Well, you inspector of lanterns. Have corpses hung in the street given France enlightenment?

3RD PRISONER. Let him alone. Those lips said the word 'mercy'.

PHILIPPEAU. 'Mercy?' Oh yes. We are priests who prayed with the dying. We caught their disease and now we die of it.

SEVERAL VOICES. The blow that strikes you, kills all of us.

CAMILLE. Gentlemen, I apologise. Our efforts were fruitless. Now I go to the scaffold because my eyes watered at the fate of a few unhappy men.

Scene Two

A room.

FOUQUIER-TINVILLE, HERMAN.

FOUQUIER. Everything ready?

HERMAN. It's going to be hard. If Danton weren't among them, there'd be no problem.

FOUQUIER. He must lead the dance.

HERMAN. He'll frighten the jury. He's the Revolution's scarecrow.

FOUQUIER. The jury must say 'Guilty'.

HERMAN. There is a way. It's a little contemptuous of legal procedure.

FOUQUIER. Out with it.

HERMAN. We don't draw lots for the jury, we handpick our men.

FOUQUIER. That should work. It'll be a good bonfire. I've thrown in a few more accused, four forgers, a couple of pimps, a few bankers and foreigners. A tasty dish, just what the people need. Right. Reliable jurors. Who?

HERMAN. Leroi, he's deaf. He never hears anything the defendant's say. Danton can shout himself hoarse there.

FOUQUIER. Who else?

HERMAN. Vilatte, our resident alcoholic and Lumiere who sleeps all the time. Just kick them and they'll yell 'Guilty!' Then Girard, who works on the principle that anyone who appears before the tribunal is automatically condemned. Then Renaudin —

FOUQUIER. Him? He once helped priests escape.

HERMAN. Don't worry. He came to see me a few days ago. He demanded that all condemned men be bled from the veins to tone them down a bit, he doesn't like their defiant attitude.

FOUQUIER. Excellent. So, I depend on you.

HERMAN. Just leave it to me.

Scene Three

The Conciergerie. A corridor. LACROIX, DANTON, MERCIER *and other* PRISONERS, *pacing up and down.*

LACROIX (*to one of the* PRISONERS). How can there be so many in these wretched circumstances?

PRISONER. Didn't the tumbrils tell you? Paris is a butcher's block.

MERCIER. You know all about it, Lacroix. Equality waves its sickle over its head, the lava of the Revolution flows, the guillotine makes us all republicans, no? And the gallery claps and the Romans rub their hands. But they don't hear that every word they speak is the death rattle of a victim. Follow the logic of your phrases, see them become flesh and blood.

Look around you. You spoke this. This is your rhetoric, translated. These wretches, their executioners, the guillotine are your speeches come to life. You have built your doctrines out of human heads.

DANTON. You are right. Today everything is worked in human flesh. That is the curse of our age. Now my body is to be a building block. It's a year since I created the revolutionary tribunal. I ask pardon for that, from God and man. I wanted to prevent new September massacres, to save the innocent. But this slow murder, with its grotesque formalities, is more hideous than what went before. Gentlemen, I hoped to free you.

MERCIER. Oh, we'll be free all right.

DANTON. Now I find . . . I myself sharing your predicament. And I do not know how it will end.

Scene Four

The Revolutionary Tribunal.

HERMAN (*to* DANTON). Your name citizen?

DANTON. The Revolution knows my name, it is in the pantheon of history. As for my place of residence, that will soon be the void.

HERMAN. Danton. The convention accuses you of having conspired with Mirabeau, with Dumouriez, with Orléans, with the Girondins, the foreigners and the faction of Louis XVII.

DANTON. My voice, which rang out so often in the people's cause, will refute these slanders. Let the scum who accuse me come here and I will heap shame on them. Call the Committees to the tribunal. I will answer only before them. They are my prosecutors and my witnesses. Call them! Make them show themselves! Besides, what do you and your verdict matter to me? I've told you. The void will soon be my sanctuary. Life is a burden, take it from me, I will be glad.

HERMAN. Danton. Bravado is the mark of guilt, composure a sign of innocence.

DANTON. Bravado is, no doubt, a fault. But that national bravado, the bravado of defiance with which I fought for liberty, that is the greatest of all virtues. I invoke that sense of daring, that defiance now, in the name of the republic and against my accusers. What composure can there be from me when I find myself slandered and calumnied? I am a revolutionary. You cannot expect a cool and modest defence from my kind. Men of my stamp are beyond price to the Revolution, the genius of liberty shines from our brows.

Signs of applause among the listeners.

I am accused of conspiring with Mirabeau, with Dumouriez, with Orléans, of crawling at the feet of wretched despots. I am summoned to answer before inexorable and unswerving justice. I, I am!

St Just, you miserable man, you will answer to posterity for this slander!

HERMAN. I demand your answer calmly. Remember, Marat showed respect to his judges.

DANTON. They have laid hands on my whole life. Let it stand up, let it fight back! I will bury them beneath the weight of all my deeds.

I am not arrogant about what I have done. Fate guides everyone's arm. But only a mighty personality can be fate's instrument.

On the Champs de Mars I declared war on the Monarchy, on the 10th of August I attacked it, on the 21st of January I killed it and threw down a King's head, a gauntlet to all monarchs.

Repeated signs of applause. He picks up the indictment.

I glance at this scandalous tissue of lies. My whole being is shaken. Who are they, who had to force Danton into the Champs de Mars? Who are these wondrous beings from whom he had to steal his strength? Let my accusers appear! I know what I do when I make that demand. I will tear the mask from these villains and hurl them back into the darkness, from which they should never have crawled.

HERMAN (*rings a bell*). Don't you hear the bell?

DANTON. The voice of a man defending his honour and his life drowns your bell!

In September I fed the young brood of the Revolution with morsels of aristocrat flesh. My voice forged weapons for the people from the gold of the rich and the aristocracy. My voice was the hurricane that drowned the lackeys of the despots under waves of bayonets.

Loud applause.

HERMAN. Danton, your voice is cracked. Conclude your defence later. The session is closed.

DANTON. Now you see me! A few more hours and Danton will die in the arms of glory!

Scene Five

The Luxembourg: a dungeon.

DILLON, LAFLOTTE, *a* GAOLER.

DILLON. Don't poke your nose in my face like that! (*Laughs.*)

LAFLOTTE. And don't poke your mouth in mine. Ugh, a
crescent moon with a stinking halo. (*Laughs.*)

GAOLER. Think you can read by its light, sir?

He indicates a newspaper in his hand.

DILLON. Give me that.

GAOLER. Sorry General, my moon is very low, as it were.

LAFLOTTE. It's brought on a flood, to judge by the state of
your trousers.

GAOLER. No, low tide, low tide. (*To* DILLON.) Give me
something to make it bright, if you want to read, General.

DILLON. Here. Now go away. (*He gives him money.*)

The GAOLER *goes off.*

(DILLON *reads.*) Danton frightens the tribunal, the jury
divided, the assembly unhappy. Extraordinary crowds,
packed around the Palais de Justice, all the way back to the
bridges. Oh, for a handful of gold to buy my way out of
here, eh? (*He paces up and down, occasionally pouring
himself a drink.*) If I could get one foot in the street, I'd
not let myself be slaughtered like this. One foot in the
street!

LAFLOTTE. Or in a tumbril. Same thing.

DILLON. There'd be a few steps one to the other, to tread on a
few Decemvir corpses. It's time decent people stood up to
be counted.

LAFLOTTE (*aside*). Stood up to be guillotined. Come on you
old fool, drink yourself stupid.

DILLON. Idiots! They'll end up guillotining themselves.

LAFLOTTE (*aside*). You grow to love life like your own child. As if you gave yourself the gift of life. Ha! Wonderful, to commit incest with fate and father yourself. A lucky Oedipus.

DILLON. You can't feed the people with corpses. The wives of Danton and Camille must throw paper money to the people.

LAFLOTTE (*aside*). But I won't put out my eyes, I'll need them to weep for the great General here.

DILLON. Arrest Danton. Who can be safe now? Fear will unite his attackers.

LAFLOTTE (*aside*). The old fool's damned already. What does it matter if I tread on a corpse to climb out of the grave?

DILLON. Let me get in the street. Get men, ex-soldiers, Girondins, former nobles. Break open the prisons, win the prisoners to our cause.

LAFLOTTE (*aside*). I'm going to denounce him. A flirtation with evil, and why not? I've been too narrow minded up to now. I may suffer the pangs of conscience but that will make a change from smelling my own stench. I'm bored waiting for the guillotine, I go over it twenty times a day, the reality of having my head cut off has become banal. Betrayal is more spicey.

DILLON. We must get a letter to Danton's wife.

LAFLOTTE (*aside*). It's not death I fear, it's pain. They say it's over in a second, but pain has a finer measurement of time, it can split a fraction of a second. No, pain is the only sin and suffering the only vice. Therefore I will remain virtuous.

DILLON. Hey, Laflotte! Where's the man gone? I've got money. We'll strike while the iron is hot. My plan is made.

LAFLOTTE. I'm just coming! I know the warder, I'll talk to him. Count on me, General, we'll get out of this hole. (*To himself as he goes off.*) Me into the big wide hole called the world, he into the narrow one called the grave.

Scene Six

The Committee of Public Safety. BARÈRE, ST JUST, COLLOT
D'HERBOIS, BILLAUD-VARENNES.

BARÈRE. What does Fouquier write?

ST JUST. The second hearing is over. The prisoners demanded
that certain members of the Convention and the Committee
of Public Safety appear. They appealed to the people on the
grounds that witnesses were being with-held. The emotion
was indescribable. Danton was like a parody of Jupiter,
roaring and shaking his locks.

COLLOT. All the better for Samson to grab hold of them.

BARÈRE. We must stay out of sight. The fishwives and rag
and bone men may not be so impressed by the look of us.

BILLAUD. The people relish being crushed, even by Danton
just staring at them. The insolence of it. A face like that is
more vicious than an aristocrat's coat of arms, it is an
emblem of sneering misanthropy. A face to be smashed by
anyone who refuses to be looked down upon with contempt.

BARÈRE. He's cast himself as a hero, an iron-clad Siegfried. The
blood of the September victims has made him invulnerable.
What does Robespierre say?

ST JUST. Nothing. He seems about to speak, but doesn't. The
jury must announce they have all the evidence they need and
adjourn.

BARÈRE. Impossible.

ST JUST. They must be destroyed! By any means, even if we
have to throttle them with out own bare hands. Dare! Dare!
Danton taught us that word, we must be true to it. The
revolution won't stumble over their corpses, but if Danton
hangs onto her robe — there is something in his face that
tells me he'd ravish Liberty itself, to stay alive.

ST JUST *is called outside.*

A WARDER *enters.*

WARDER. There are prisoners in Sainte-Pélagie who are dying. They ask for a doctor.

BILLAUD. Unnecessary. Less work for the executioner.

WARDER. There are pregnant women among them.

BILLAUD. Good. Their children won't need coffins.

BARÈRE. One aristocrat with consumption saves the Revolutionary Tribunal a session. Medicine would be counter-revolutionary.

COLLOT (*takes a piece of paper*). A petition. A woman's name.

BARÈRE. Ah, one more forced to choose between the boards of the guillotine or the bed of a Jacobin. Let her die dishonoured like Lucrece, but somewhat later than the Roman lady — of child-birth, or cancer, or old age. It can't be too disagreeable a duty, to drive a Tarquin out of the virtuous republic of a virginal body.

COLLOT. She's too old for that. Madame begs for death. And eloquently: she says prison lies on her like the coffin's lid. She's only been there four weeks! The simple answer? (*He writes and reads out*:) 'Madame, you have not longed for death long enough'.

The WARDER *goes off.*

BARÈRE. Collot, the guillotine must not become the butt of jokes. The people will lose their fear of it. We must not be familiar.

ST JUST *returns.*

ST JUST. I have just received a denunciation. There is a conspiracy in the prisons. A young man called Laflotte was held in the same room as Dillon. Dillon was drunk and talked.

BARÈRE. People have cut their throats on a bottle before.

ST JUST. The plot is that the wives of Danton and Camille will throw the people money. Dillon is to escape, free the prisoners and, with them, storm the Convention.

BARÈRE. Fairy tales.

ST JUST. A fairy tale to send them to sleep. Evidence of
treason! Add to that the insolence of the accused, the
discontent of the people, the confusion of the jury, and —.
I'll write an official report.

BARÈRE. Do that, St Just, spin your sentences. Every comma
the cut of a sabre, every full-stop a severed head.

ST JUST. The Convention must issue a decree that the Tribunal
will continue its hearings without interruptions. And that
it has the right to exclude any of the accused who act in
contempt of the court or create a disturbance.

BARÈRE. You have the revolutionary's tactical instinct. A
moderate demand to achieve an extreme effect. They can't
be silent, Danton will have to cry out.

ST JUST. I count on your support. There are those in the
Convention who grow as diseased as Danton. They fear the
same remedy. Their courage has returned, they are certain
to protest against the flouting of procedure —

BARÈRE (*interrupting him*). I'll tell them that: in Rome the
consul who discovered the Catiline conspiracy and executed
the criminals on the spot was accused of flouting procedure.
And who were his accusers?

COLLOT (*emotionally*). Go, St Just! The lava of revolution
flows. Liberty will strangle in her embrace those weaklings
who dreamt they could fertilise her mighty womb. The
people will appear in thunder and lightning, like Jupiter to
Semele, and burn them to ash. Go, St Just, we will hurl
down the thunderbolt upon the cowards' heads.

ST JUST *goes off.*

BARÈRE. Did you hear the word 'remedy'? Now they're
making the guillotine a cure for the pox. They're not fighting
the moderates, they're fighting vice.

BILLAUD. We've gone along with it. So far.

BARÈRE. But Robespierre wants to make the revolution a
lecture hall for morality. He uses the guillotine as a pulpit.

BILLAUD. Or a prayer stool.

COLLOT. Let him put his head on it, not his knees.

BARÈRE. Anything can happen now. The world is topsy-turvy. Virtue turns murderer, criminals die like saints.

COLLOT (*to* BARÈRE). When are you coming to the house at Clichy again?

BARÈRE. When the doctor stops calling.

COLLOT. You must think there's a comet, stationary over that place. Its scorching rays are shrivelling up your spine.

BILLAUD. Next thing, the dainty fingers of little Jacqueline will pull his spine right out of its sheath. And hang it down his back, like a pigtail.

BARÈRE (*shrugs his shoulders*). Sh! The Incorruptible mustn't know.

BILLAUD. Don't worry. He is an impotent Mahomet. He only has eyes for his mountain.

BILLAUD *and* COLLOT *go off.*

BARÈRE. You monster. 'You have not longed for death long enough.' The words should have severed the tongue that spoke them.

And what, what about me?

When the Septembrists burst into the prisons, one of the prisoners had a penknife. He pushed in among the assassins and stabbed a priest, in the heart, right in front of them. That way he saved his skin.

And why not?

Do I now rush in amongst the assassins of the Committee of Public Safety and grab the blade of the guillotine?

Why not? We are all prisoners at the feet of assassins, murdering each other. And if it is moral to kill one to save your life, why not two? Or three? Where does it end? Huh. I'm like a child playing with barleycorns. One, two, three, four how many to make a pile? Come my conscience, come little chick, chick-chick-chick, here's food for you.

Scene Seven

The Conciergerie.

LACROIX, DANTON, PHILIPPEAU, CAMILLE.

LACROIX. You roared wonderfully Danton. If you'd strained
yourself like that earlier, we'd not be in this state now. But
death makes you yell, eh? Coming closer and closer to your
face 'til you can smell his foul breath.

CAMILLE. If only he'd over-power you at once, force what
he wants from you in hot-blood, not like this, with all the
formalities. It's like marrying an old woman. The articles
are drawn up, witnesses are called, the register signed and
blotted — then into your bed she slowly crawls with her
cold arms.

DANTON. Yes. I wish it were a fight, tooth and nail. But I've
fallen into a mill, my limbs are being ground off, systematically.
I am being killed by a cold, mechanical power.

CAMILLE. You lie there alone. Stiff. Cold. In the clammy
swamp of putrefaction. Perhaps death draws the life from
your fibres slowly, but you're fully awake! Even in the
grave, you feel life ebb away.

PHILIPPEAU. Don't worry, my friends. Think of the autumn
crocuses, that don't bear seeds 'til winter's gone. We're like
flowers being transplanted, except when it's done to us we
tend to stink a bit.

DANTON. Huh. An edifying prospect: to be transplanted from
one dung heap to the next. Remember the classification of
the world drummed into us at school? From primary to
secondary, from secondary to tertiary etcetera etcetera? Bah,
I've had enough of sitting on school benches, my behind's as
sore as a baboon's.

PHILIPPEAU. So what do you want?

DANTON. Peace.

PHILIPPEAU. Peace is in God.

DANTON. In nothingness. What greater peace can there be to lose yourself in? If God's peace is the greatest, then God is nothingness, huh? But I am an atheist. I have to believe atheism's cursèd argument: nothing that exists can cease to exist, something cannot become nothing. And I am something, more's the pity.

Creation has spread itself so wide there is nowhere left empty. Everything swarms and seethes. The void has murdered itself, creation is its wound, we are its drops of blood, the world is the grave in which it rots. That sounds mad but there's a truth there.

CAMILLE. The world is the wandering Jew. Death is nothingness but nothingness is impossible. 'Oh never more to die', as the song goes.

DANTON. We're buried alive. Pharoahs, in three or four-layered coffins, the sky, our houses, our shirts and our jackets.

We scratch for fifty years on the lid of the coffin. Oh yes, he who could believe in annihilation, he would indeed be saved.

Life is just a more complex, a more ordered putrefaction than the simple rotting of death. But that's the only difference, complexity, otherwise life and death are one and the same.

Still! I've got so used to decay in life I don't want to cope with the other sort. Julie. To die without her. Even if I am destroyed utterly, powdered into a handful of martyred dust, utterly, without her not one atom will have peace. I can't die. No. I can't die. I'll cry out. Let them wring every drop of blood from me.

Scene Eight

A room.

FOUQUIER, AMAR, VOLAND.

FOUQUIER. I don't know what to do. Now they are
  demanding a commission of enquiry.

AMAR. Then we've got the bastards. Here you are. (*He hands*
  FOUQIER *a paper.*)

VOULAND. That'll do it.

FOUQUIER. Yes. Yes. Just what we need.

AMAR. Let's do it. End it now. For us and for them.

Scene Nine

The Revolutionary Tribunal

DANTON. The Republic is in danger and the President of the
  tribunal has no brief! We appeal to the people. My voice is
  still strong. I will pronounce a funeral oration over the
  Decemvirs. I repeat: we demand a commission of enquiry.
  We have important disclosures to make. I will withdraw into
  the fortress of reason. I will unleash the cannons of truth
  and crush my enemies.

  Signs of applause.
  Enter FOUQUIER, AMAR, VOULAND.

FOUQUIER. Silence in the name of the Republic! The
  Convention issues the following decree. In consideration
  of signs of mutiny in the prisons; in consideration that the
  wives of Danton and Camille throw money to the people;
  in consideration that there is a conspiracy for General
  Dillon to escape and lead insurgents in an attempt to free
  the accused; and, finally, in consideration that the accused
  have created disturbances designed to bring the tribunal
  into disrepute, the tribunal is hereby empowered to
  continue its investigations without interruption and to

exclude from the debate any of the accused who make light of the respect due to the law.

DANTON. I ask you, have we spoken in contempt of the tribunal, or the people, or the Convention?

MANY VOICES. No! No!

CAMILLE. The bastards! They want to murder my wife.

DANTON. One day men will know the truth. I see a great disaster overwhelming France. It is dictatorship, it has torn off its veil, it holds its head high, it tramples over corpses. (*Pointing at* AMAR *and* VOLAND.) There are the assassins, the ravens of the Committee of Public Safety.

I accuse Robespierre, St Just and their executioners of high treason.

They want to choke the Republic in blood. The ruts made by the tumbrils are the highways on which foreign armies will flood into the heart of France.

How long must the footprints of liberty be graves?

You want bread, they throw you heads. You are thirsty, they make you lick the steps of the guillotines.

Violent commotion in the assembly — shouts of applause.

MANY VOICES. Long live Danton, down with the Decemvirs!

The PRISONERS *are forcibly removed.*

Scene Ten

A street.

A FEW VOICES. Down with the Decemvirs! Long live Danton!

1ST CITIZEN. Bread not heads, wine not blood!

SOME WOMEN. The guillotine's a bad flour mill, Samson's a rotten baker's boy, we want bread, bread!

2ND CITIZEN. Danton's head will give you bread again.

1ST CITIZEN. Danton was with us on the 10th of August,
    Danton was with us in September. Where were his accusers?

2ND CITIZEN. Lafayette was with you at Versailles and yet he
    was a traitor.

1ST CITIZEN. Who says Danton is a traitor?

2ND CITIZEN. Robespierre.

1ST CITIZEN. Robespierre is a traitor.

2ND CITIZEN. Who says?

1ST CITIZEN. Danton.

2ND CITIZEN. Danton has fine clothes, Danton has a fine house,
    Danton has a fine wife, Danton bathes in burgundy, eats
    venison off silver plates, Danton sleeps with your wives and
    daughters when he's drunk.

    Danton was poor like you, where did he get it all?
    — The king gave it to him, to save his crown.
    — The Duke of Orleans bribed him to steal the throne for him.
    — The foreigners gave it to him to betray you all.
    — What's Robespierre got? Nothing but virtue. Virtuous
    Robespierre! You all know him.

ALL. Long live Robespierre! Down with Danton! Down with the
    traitor!

Act Four

Scene One

A room.

JULIE, *a* BOY.

JULIE. It's over. They trembled before him. Now they're
killing him out of fear. Go, I've seen him for the last time.
I don't want to see him like that.

She gives him a lock of hair.

There. Take him that and tell him he won't go alone. He'll
understand. Then come back quickly, I want to read his look
in your eyes.

Scene Two

DUMAS, *a* CITIZEN.

CITIZEN. How can they condemn so many to death after a
hearing like that?

DUMAS. It is unusual. But the men of the Revolution have an
instinct that others lack.

CITIZEN. The instinct of the tiger. I — heard about your wife.

DUMAS. My wife. Yes. Soon I will be a widower.

CITIZEN. Then it's true? You denounced her?

DUMAS. The revolutionary tribunal will announce our divorce.
The guillotine will grant a decree nisi.

CITIZEN. You're a monster!

DUMAS. You simpleton. Do you admire Brutus?

CITIZEN. With all my heart.

DUMAS. Then you, like a Roman Consul, hide your head in your toga when you sacrifice what is nearest and dearest to you. I just rub my eyes with the sleeve of my red jacket. That's the only difference between us.

CITIZEN. That's horrific.

DUMAS. Go away. You don't understand me.

Scene Three

The Conciergerie. LACROIX, HÉRAULT (*on one bed*), DANTON, CAMILLE (*on another*).

LACROIX. Your hair! It gets so long. And your nails, you're ashamed of them.

HÉRAULT. Don't sneeze. Dust gets in my eyes.

LACROIX. And don't tread on my feet. I've got corns.

HÉRAULT. And lice.

LACROIX. It's not the lice I think about, it's the worms.

HÉRAULT. Well, with that thought, goodnight. Sleep well my friend. And could you not tug at this corpse's winding sheet? It's cold.

DANTON. Yes, Camille. Tomorrow we'll be worn out shoes, thrown to that old beggar woman, the earth.

CAMILLE. Nothing but the leather slippers, Plato said the angels patter round the earth in.

DANTON. Stop worrying, boy.

CAMILLE. They can't touch her. The light of her beauty that flows from her body is inextinguishable, it will burn them. Impossible! See, the earth won't dare bury her, it will form an arch above her, the vapours of the grave will sparkle on her eye lashes like dew, crystals will grow like flowers about her sweet limbs and springs, from deep in the earth, will murmur to her.

DANTON. Sh, boy. Sleep now.

CAMILLE. Danton. Tell me. Secretly. Dying's just pain isn't it? It achieves nothing. I want to look into life's beautiful eyes a little longer.

DANTON. Your eyes'll be open, like it or not. The executioner doesn't bother to close eyelids. Sleep is more merciful. Try to sleep.

CAMILLE. Yes. Lucile fantasies on my lips. A dream, safe inside.

DANTON. Will the clock never stop? With each tick the walls close in on me. Narrow as a coffin. I read a story like that when I was a child. My hair stood on end.

When I was a child. All that effort to feed and clothe me, keep me warm, just to make work for the gravediggers. I feel I'm already stinking. Dear body, I'll hold my nose and pretend you are a woman, sweaty from dancing, and whisper to you. We had some times, you and I, body.

Tomorrow you'll be a broken fiddle, your tune played out. An empty bottle, the wine drunk. But I'll go sober to bed. Lucky people who can still get drunk! A crumpled pair of stinking trousers you'll be, body, thrown in the wardrobe. The moths will eat you up. Huh, this doesn't do any good. Yes, dying is pain. Death apes birth. We go to it naked and helpless babies. We get a winding sheet for swaddling clothes, but what comfort that? We whimper in the grave as we did in the cradle. Camille? Asleep. (*As he leans over him.*) His eyelids are flickering. A dream. The golden dew of sleep.

He rises and goes to the window.

Thank you, Julie. I won't go alone. But I'd like to have died differently. Effortlessly, the way a star falls, a note of music ends, a ray of light is lost in clear water.

The stars prick the night like tears. There must be great grief in the eye that shed them.

CAMILLE. Oh! (*He has sat up and is groping toward the roof.*)

DANTON. Camille, what's wrong?

CAMILLE. Oh, oh —

DANTON (*shakes him*). Do you want to tear the roof down?

CAMILLE. You! Speak!

DANTON. You're shivering and sweating.

CAMILLE. It's you. Me. My hand. I know where I am. Danton, it was horrible.

DANTON. What was?

CAMILLE. I was half awake, half dreaming. Then the roof disappeared. The moon sank down right to my face. The roof of heaven had fallen. I hammered at it, I scratched at the stars. I was a drowning man, under a roof of ice. Horrible.

DANTON. The lamp throws a round refection on the ceiling. That's what you saw.

CAMILLE. I tell you, I see it takes nothing to lose the little reason we have. (*He stands.*) I won't sleep anymore.

He picks up a book.

DANTON. What's that?

CAMILLE. Young's *Night Thoughts.*

DANTON. Huh! You want a literary death before the real thing? Me, I'll read Voltaire's *The Virgin*. I don't want to slide out of life from a church pew. I'll go from the bed of a sister of mercy. Life is a whore that fornicates with all the world.

Scene Four

The square in front of the Conciergerie.

A PRISON WARDER, *two* CARTERS *with tumbrils*, WOMEN.

WARDER. Who's called you here?

1ST CARTER. You here? That's a funny name.

WARDER. A joker. Who gave you authority to pull in here?

1ST CARTER. Just private enterprise. I get ten sous a head.

2ND CARTER. Oy! This is my run. The bastard wants to take the bread from my mouth.

1ST CARTER. They your bread then? (*Pointing to the prisoners at the window.*) They look more like bait for worms.

2ND CARTER. Well my kids are little worms too and want their share. What a way to earn a living. And we are the best carters around.

1ST CARTER. How do you make that out?

2ND CARTER. What makes a good carter?

1ST CARTER. He who goes furtherest and fastest.

2ND CARTER. So who goes further than a man leaving this world? And who goes faster than a man who does it in a quarter of an hour? Which is what it takes from here to the Place de la Revolution.

WARDER. Come on, move up to the gate! Let them through, ladies.

1ST CARTER. Go straight through the middle and straight up that lot.

2ND CARTER. Drive a coach and horses right through. A well rutted track. Mind you, you'd be in quarantine when you came out again.

They drive forward.

(*To the* WOMEN.) What are you gawping at?

WOMAN. Waiting for old customers.

2ND CARTER. Think this cart's a brothel? This is a highly respectable cart. It's carried aristocrats, this cart, all the way to their last supper.

LUCILE *enters, sits on a stone under the* PRISONERS' *window.*

LUCILE. Camille, Camille! Camille, you look so funny. You've got a stone coat on. That iron mask on your face. And where are your arms? Why don't you move? I'll make you.

(*Sings*):
Two stars in the sky
Brighter than the moon
One at the window one at the door
Of my true love's room.

Sh. Come on. They're asleep. Up the stairs. The moon's
made me wait too long. You can't get in the door! You're
wearing stones. Stones. Bars. A cruel joke, to wear those
heavy clothes. You're not even moving. You frighten me.

Listen to me! Don't pull that face, long door-with-locks face.
Death has a long face. Death, what word's that, Camille?
Oh look, it's there. Hey, hey, I'll catch it. Help me. Come,
come, come —

She runs off.

CAMILLE (*calls*). Lucile! Lucile!

Scene Five

The Conciergerie. DANTON *at a window giving onto the next
room.* CAMILLE, PHILIPPEAU, LACROIX, HÉRAULT.

DANTON. You calmer now, Fabre, my poet?

VOICE (*from within*). At death. Thank you.

DANTON. You know what we're going to do now?

FABRE. What?

DANTON. What you've done all your life. Worm out rotten verses.

CAMILLE. Lucile was out there. Madness sat behind her eyes.
But many are mad now, that's the way the world is going.
What can we do about it? Nothing. Better to wash our
hands of it and turn away.

DANTON. I'm leaving everything in a terrible mess. Who will be
left who knows anything at all about government? They
might get by if I leave Robespierre my whores and Couthon
my shapely legs.

LACROIX. They say we made Liberty a whore.

DANTON. Which it always was! Liberty and whores are the most cosmopolitan things under the sun. Let her go and prostitute herself in virtuous marriage with the lawyer of Arras.

But she'll be Clytemnestra to him. I give him six months before I drag him down with me.

CAMILLE (*to himself*). Heaven send her sweet delusions. The greatest delusion is reason itself. The happiest man alive is he who believes in the Father, Son and Holy Ghost.

LACROIX. I look forward to the fools crying 'Long Live the Republic' as we go by.

DANTON. What does it matter? Let the storm of the Revolution wash up our corpses where it will. People will break open the heads of kings with our fossilised bones.

CAMILLE. Yes. If there's a Samson to wield our jawbones.

LACROIX. Robespierre is a Nero. Look how friendly he was to Camille just before he had him arrested.

CAMILLE. If you say so. What's it to me? What a lovely child she's given birth to, out of her madness. Why must I go now? I could have played with her, cradled her.

DANTON. When history comes to open its tombs, despots may yet choke on the stench of our corpses.

HÉRAULT. We stank pretty high in our lives, too. You're talking to posterity Danton, not to us at all.

CAMILLE. He puts on a face to be dug up in stone by the archeologists of the future.

All that effort, pursing your lips, painting your face, putting on a good accent. We should take off our masks. Then we'll see, like in a room of mirrors, only the infinitely repeated, age-old image of the fool, the joker's head. We are very like each other. All villains and angels, idiots and geniuses, all things in one. We all sleep, digest food, make children, we are all variations in different keys on the same tune. That's why

we strut about, put on faces: we embarrass one another
because we know each other so well. And now that we've all
eaten ourselves sick at the same time don't let's hold napkins
up to our mouths and pretend we've not got belly-ache.
Yell and groan as it takes you. No heroic gestures, no witty
sallies. Spare yourselves the trouble. We all know each other.

HÉRAULT. Yes, Camille, let's sit down and scream. Why be
tight-lipped when you're in pain? Greeks and Gods screamed
aloud, Romans and Stoics pulled the heroic faces.

DANTON. Greek or Roman, they were all Epicureans, like the
rest of us. They did what made them feel impressive. Why
not drape your toga about you and cast a long shadow? Why
torment ourselves? All to decide whether we hide our shame
with the paraphernalia of laurel-leaves and rose garlands, or
whether we just leave the horrid thing bare to be licked by
dogs.

PHILIPPEAU. My friends. Stand a little above the earth and
you lose sight of the mad bustle of the world to see the
sweeping lines of God's great design. To his ear the clashes
and cries that deafen us are a torrent of harmonies.

DANTON. But we are the poor musicians and our bodies are
our instruments. Are the hideous sounds torn from us only
notes to drift up and up and dwindle and die as a sensual
breath in heavenly ears?

HÉRAULT. Are we suckling pigs for princely tables, whipped
to death with rods to make our flesh more tasty?

DANTON. Are the flames that roast we children in Moloch's
furnace only feathers of light, that the Gods tickle us with
to enjoy our laughter?

CAMILLE. Is the ether a goldfish bowl, set on the table before
the blessed Gods, and do the Gods laugh eternally and rejoice
eternally enjoying the play of colour in the death agony?

DANTON. The world is chaos. It will give birth to a god called
'Nothingness'.

The WARDER *enters.*

WARDER. Gentlemen. Your carriages are at the door.

PHILIPPEAU. Goodnight, my friends. Let's go to bed and pull the great blanket, beneath which hearts stop and eyes close, over us.

They embrace each other.

HÉRAULT. Cheer up, Camille. It's a clear evening, it'll be a fine night. The last rays of the sun are on Olympus. The Gods pale and fade.

They go off.

Scene Six

A room.

JULIE. People were running in the street. Now it's quiet.

She takes out a phial.

Dear priest. Your amen sends us to bed.

She goes to the window.

It's lovely to say goodbye. I've only to pull the door behind me.

She drinks.

I'd like to stand here, always. The sun's gone. The earth stood out so sharply in the light. Now it's still as a grave. The earth is a dying woman. The light is beautiful on her face.

She grows paler and paler.

She drifts, her clothes are heavy, spread wide. Will no one pull her from the stream and bury her? Sh. I'll go. Not a kiss, not a breath to wake her.

Sleep. Sleep.

Scene Seven

The Place de la Revolution. The tumbrils arrive and stop in front of the guillotine.

MEN *and* WOMEN *dance and sing the Carmagnole.*

The PRISONERS *strike up the Marseillaise.*

A WOMAN *with* CHILDREN. Get out the way! The children are hungry and crying. I want to let them watch to keep them quiet. Get out!

A WOMAN. Hey, Danton! Now you can fornicate with the worms.

ANOTHER WOMAN. Hérault, I'll make me a wig out of your pretty hair.

HÉRAULT. I've not got enough for your bald head.

CAMILLE. Witches! You'll quote the Bible in the end: 'Fall on us, ye mountains.'

WOMAN. The mountain's fallen on you now.

DANTON (*to* CAMILLE). Calm down my boy, you've shouted yourself hoarse.

CAMILLE (*gives the* CARTER *money*). There you are, Charon. Make your cart a good serving dish. Gentlemen, I'll be carved first. It's a classical feast. We recline in our places and spill a little blood, as a libation. Goodbye, Danton.

He ascends the scaffold.

The PRISONERS *follow him, one after another.*

DANTON *goes last.*

LACROIX (*to the* PEOPLE). You kill us on the day you lost your reason. On the day you regain it, you will kill them.

SEVERAL VOICES. We've heard that one before. Boring, boring!

LACROIX. The tyrants will break their necks on the edge of my grave.

HÉRAULT (*to* DANTON). Pompous ass. He thinks his corpse will be a compost heap to ferment liberty.

PHILIPPEAU. I forgive you all. I hope your hour of death will be no more bitter than mine.

HÉRAULT. There he goes. Tearing at his heart to show the people down there he's got a clean shirt on.

FABRE. Goodbye Danton. I die a double death.

DANTON. Adieu my friend. Death is the best doctor.

HÉRAULT (*tries to embrace* DANTON). I can't joke any more. It's time.

An EXECUTIONER *pushes him back.*

DANTON (*to the* EXECUTIONER). Will you be crueller than death? Will you stop our heads kissing in the basket?

Scene Eight

LUCILE. And yet there's something in it. I begin to understand.

Death, death —

Everything has the right to live. That gnat. That bird. So why not him? The stream of life should stop if a single drop is spilt. The earth should be wounded. Everything moves, clocks go, bells ring, people walk, water runs, everything goes on and on, then — No. it can't happen. I'll sit down on the ground and scream so everything will stand still, in shock. Everything stock-still.

She sits down, covers her eyes and screams.

After a pause, she stands.

No good, everything as before, the houses, the street, the wind blows, clouds move. We just have to bear it.

Some WOMEN *come down the street.*

1ST WOMAN. A good-looking man, that Hérault.

2ND WOMAN. The way he stood by the Arc de Triomphe at the Festival of the Convention, I thought then 'he'll look good on the guillotine'. It was a premonition.

3RD WOMAN. Yes. You need to see people when they're up

and when they're down. It's good they've made death so public.

They move on.

LUCILE. Camille, where shall I look for you now?

Scene Nine

Two EXECUTIONERS *busy with the guillotine.*

1ST EXECUTIONER (*stands by the guillotine and sings*).
      Homeward I go
      In the moonlight's glow —

2ND EXECUTIONER. Hey, you done yet?

1ST EXECUTIONER. Hang on. (*Sings:*)
      Oh sister moon
      Why linger long and low

There we are. Give me my jacket.

They go off, singing.

Homeward I go
In the moonlight's glow.

LUCILE (*enters and sits on the steps of the guillotine*). I sit
on your lap, silent angel of death. (*Sings.*)
      There is a reaper name of Death
      Who draws breath
      From Almighty God.

Dear cradle who rocked Camille asleep. You suffocated
him under your roses. You passing bell, your sweet tongue
sang him to his grave. (*Sings:*)
      Men and women, short and tall
      Countless thousands fall
      Down before your scythe.

A PATROL enters.

A CITIZEN. Who's there?

LUCILE. Long live the King!

CITIZEN. In the name of the Republic.

She is surrounded by the WATCH *and led away.*